THREE POETS AND REALITY

STUDY OF
A GERMAN, AN AUSTRIAN, AND A SWISS
CONTEMPORARY LYRICIST

BY RUTH J. HOFRICHTER

ASSOCIATE PROFESSOR OF GERMAN

VASSAR COLLEGE

Published for Vassar College

NEW HAVEN

YALE UNIVERSITY PRESS

LONDON · HUMPHREY MILFORD · OXFORD UNIVERSITY PRESS

1942

The Printing-Office of the Yale University Press

*The Publication
of this book was made possible
by the
Lucy Maynard Salmon Fund
for Research
Established at Vassar College
in 1926*

ACKNOWLEDGMENT

It is a pleasure to express my gratitude to the many friends and colleagues who have helped me greatly with this book. I desire to thank in particular the members of the Department of German at Vassar College, especially Professor Lilian L. Stroebe, and members of the Faculty Committee on Research, especially Professor Amy Reed, for their friendly advice; Mr. Kenneth Porter for his constructive criticism of the verse translations, and Miss Annabel Learned for valuable assistance in developing the argument and polishing the writing.

Research for the study was made possible by a grant of the Ottendorffer Fellowship from Bryn Mawr College in 1929–30, and of the Faculty Fellowship from Vassar College, 1938–39.

CONTENTS

INTRODUCTION

THE present study was prompted by a desire to compare two aspects of a poet's world. On the one hand, his philosophy: that is to say, his consciously conceived image of the world, together with his ideals and the contribution he wishes to make to his time—everything that is implied in the word *Weltanschauung*; this I hoped to establish first. On the other hand, I wanted to look at the image of the world as it emerges in the poet's work itself: what landscapes does he describe, and in what terms? What colors and what moods does he prefer? How does he see human beings, and what creatures attract him? And is there a significance back of his choice?

In exploring these aspects of his work, one might hope to see what harmony or discrepancy prevails in the poet's being; whether there is any conflict between his consciously conceived Weltanschauung and the image of the world brought forth by a spontaneous imagination from sources other than his conscious mind. The poet chosen for this exploration was Hans Carossa —for no better reason than a predilection for his fine and delicate art, and the wish to understand it better.

However, as the study proceeded another question presented itself. Carossa had chosen to stay in Germany at a time when most writers of eminence left the country. Yet the closer my acquaintance with his work, the more I felt the deep integrity of the man. What, then, made it possible for this writer not merely to remain under a regime which others found deadly to their art, but to remain as a poet honored by the National

Socialist Government, which demands conformity from all who live and produce within its realm?

There are several possibilities open to an author faced with these circumstances. He may revolt against the regime—and this may seem to him the only fulfillment possible, whether poetic or human. What will be the result? If not death or prison, certainly exile. The effect of conditions of exile on his art, if not his life, is a separate question; we are considering here rather the conditions for one who has remained.

He may feel wholeheartedly for the regime, and give it an artist's support; this too would be a fulfillment of his poetic destiny.

He may withdraw into silence, or into a part of his mental world where the noise of the day is muted, abstracting himself from present happenings. Here he must sacrifice, in whole or in part, the creative range of his work, and suffer a cutting off or numbing of power. Or indeed, his art itself may be of a sort not to be touched by passing events.

On the other hand, the poet may feel a deep compulsion to remain close to his own people and the country of which he is a part: neither revolting, nor accepting, nor silent, but in some byway of life preserving what he can of the artistic strength of his culture. His penalties and limitations in this case will be very similar to those mentioned, but they will form a part of his work rather than a hindrance to it, for his mission will be a preservation through, and in spite of, the present, and however difficult the task, these conditions will be part of it.

For one who has not revolted, here are some of the possibilities. There are naturally others, and all manner of blending of them. Carossa did not revolt—what is his story, then? This phase of a poet's integrity becomes almost as interesting as the one first proposed. In fact, they are facets of the same thing: the poet's relation to reality.

The orientation of any human being to reality raises a variety of questions. What, for instance, has been the impact on his life of the realities of the world into which he was born? Moreover, out of this totality of experience a man will consciously or unconsciously select a certain number with which to create "his" world—what, then, has been his choice? And why? It will bear fruit, since this selection, together with the unconscious impact of the total world upon him, will determine a new reality: that which he tries to shape out of his own forces—the nature of his essential contribution to his time. In order to understand a human being we must probe into these phases of his life. And we may look for one more aspect: in the end, and at the core of things, what was he in his heart really searching for?

The answers I have found will be given in the following pages. But while the focus was at the outset more or less narrowly poetic and personal, there came to light more and more clearly certain broader implications as to the effect on a sensitive, creative mind of the powerful stream of Europe's destiny. This influence became increasingly apparent as the study was extended to other personalities.

For the sake of contrast, it seemed rewarding to consider the work of another lyricist in the same manner. The choice of Josef Weinheber, an Austrian, was dictated by the fact that like Carossa he is recognized by his contemporaries at home, as well as being very generally considered a poet of high rank—to whom among other prizes the Grosse Dichterpreis der Stadt

Wien was awarded in 1941. He also, like Carossa, chose to stay in the present Reich under the National Socialist regime.

Weinheber is a peculiar and highly individual poet. The dark and shapeless philosophy he has evolved contrasts strangely with his incredibly skilled technique and limpid form. For a time while analyzing his work I wondered whether the negative, confused content of his poetry offered anything to justify close study. However, in the end qualities emerged which appeared significant, indeed disturbingly relevant, to an understanding of the effect of general European developments upon art.

In further comparison of poetic trends in the German-speaking world, I was moved to add the analysis of a Swiss writer, of neutral background, and slightly removed from the turbulent German scene. A survey of contemporary Swiss lyricists convinced me that of this generation Albert Steffen is far and away the most significant. He lives at present close to the German border in Dornach, near Basel, as head of the Anthroposophical Society. Friends in the United States have offered to make a home for him here, but he has preferred to remain in Europe, realizing the precariousness of a European future, yet wishing to share the fate of his country whatever may be in store for him personally.

Thus we have under consideration three poets who represent, each in his fashion, the three major German-speaking groups of Europe, and who have all three remained upon their native soil during this critical moment. This line of choice was not unintentional, for I was quite definitely more interested in the experience of poets still in living touch with the culture which made them than in that of exiles, however gifted or passionately attached to their own ideals. Whatever the sincerity of the exile—and it may be very great—he does pay a definite price for his freedom: that of severing himself from mutual contact with the people, the land, and the language to which he was born. Authors whose main achievement lies in the field of the epic or the drama are often successful in another country or even another language. But the life of lyric poetry seems to be bound up with the native language of the poet. This may one day be proved a fallacy; at present I see no evidence to the contrary.

It also happens that, without reference to current issues one way or another, these men are to me, and have seemed to others, unquestionably the most significant poets of our day in German literature. Among the exiles I do not find their equal. That is to say, if somewhere in the unpolitical reaches of outer space I were confronted with all modern German-speaking poets and were asked to select the three foremost in the lyric field, I would not, in all humility, choose otherwise. I do not therefore feel that an apology is needed for the basis of selection.

Indeed, if these are the most important talents of the day, this in itself makes their experience relevant to us, as the power and sensitiveness of the poet may be eloquent, even inadvertently, for the forces of his time.

THE BACKGROUND

B Y the middle of the nineteenth century Heinrich
Heine's brilliant poetry had effectively destroyed
romanticism in Germany. No one could write in this
vein after his biting ironies. Moreover, a growing political
unrest left little scope for lyric feeling. We still have
delicate poems by the North-German Theodor Storm,
charming and nostalgic nature lyrics by Gottfried
Keller, and the austerely splendid symbolism of his
Swiss countryman, Conrad Ferdinand Meyer. These
three poets, however, are best known as writers of
short stories. Eduard Mörike, the South-German
country parson, is the only pure lyricist of the mid-
nineteenth century; his tender and glowing verses equal
the poems of Goethe's youth. But he lived apart from
the world, taking no interest in events of the day which
vitally concerned Storm and Keller.[1]

The twentieth century was ushered in by a wave of
materialism: its science based on Darwin, its social
concepts on Marx, and its art profoundly influenced by
the pseudomysticism of Richard Wagner. In literature a
number of conflicting trends become evident. Gerhart
Hauptmann,[2] though at heart an incurable romanticist,
leads the naturalistic movement. The Impressionist
school tries in vain to produce in words the elusive
effects attained on canvas by Renoir; only Hugo von
Hofmannsthal,[3] usually classed as a neoromanticist,
sometimes captures the mood of the French Impression-
ists. Expressionism, much discussed and little under-
stood, fills the years between 1910 and 1920, although
the war of 1914–18, cutting short many lives, really
deprived the movement of its natural growth and

development. It remains an unfinished symphony of young voices, stilled by sudden death. However, their efforts toward new departures were not without result. Breaking away from realism, these poets also turn from the familiar scenes of life—their landscapes move and change into clouds, or into human beings, the people they visualize are transmuted strangely into weird phantoms, or into landscapes. They dissolve the tangible world, they seek the New Man, attempting that re-valuation of all values which Nietzsche prophesied. Their eagerness to create new forms and values may be simply a reaction to the exaggerated materialism of the late nineteenth century and the beginning of the twentieth.

In analyzing the effect of Expressionism on the trend of modern lyric poetry, we find in this movement a peculiar tendency to try to tear down a reality that has lost its meaning. The poet detaches himself from time and space, and achieves this detachment by visions which create for him a new world. This may be done by dis-solving the appearance of the outer world into Impres-sionist detail, as in the poetry of such young men as Trakl[4] and Stramm;[5] the detail is not important as it would be to a genuine Impressionist, but rather serves to emphasize the futility of the life of the senses. Stramm succeeds only in shattering the coherence of outer existence as he shatters language in his explosive short poems; he does not rise to vision. Trakl, possibly the greatest talent in the group, offers instead of the visible world a lurid scene discovered behind blue mirrors, where the hermaphrodite form of the "sister" beckons, silvery and elusive. Heym,[6] another promising young man whose accidental death by drowning (1912) is strangely foreshadowed in his lyrics, also annihilates the

familiar world, to replace it by a terrible vision which
he calls Dead Eternity. In his imagination he follows a
dead girl whom he has loved; her black hair floats in the
night sky like a starry mist, and her white hands hold
the stone tears of her lover. Soon he will join her and
fill her pale hands with the lilies of his kisses. There is
no development, no future. Heym's eternity is a grue-
some material universe become completely stationary.
Werfel,[7] whose connection with Expressionism is rather
loose, seeks liberation from materialism in a dimly
conceived spiritual world drawn into the flesh.

These poets, typical of the trends within the Expres-
sionist group of lyricists, may have hoped that in
destroying old versions and perceptions of reality they
were preparing the path for others who would create
new values. The two great German lyricists of the early
twentieth century built more or less unconsciously on
this foundation, although they have their own way of
dealing with the painful clash between the arid material-
ism of modern science and the eternal hunger of the
human soul. They are Stefan George[8] and Rainer Maria
Rilke.[9]

George's volumes of lyric poems, hammered into an
almost unbelievably finished beauty of form, show a
search for a new conception of life, symbolized in the
quest for the perfect companion. In the period from 1890
to 1900 the poet seems divorced from outward reality,
seeking satisfaction in dream-visions; at times the
emperor Heliogabalus appears as the mythical friend, at
times the figure is even more shadowy. By 1907 he has
realized that the perfect friend must be the perfect
disciple. Thinly veiled, the form of a living disciple
appears in *Der siebente Ring*—it is Maximin, the
beautiful leader of a new youth. He dies but his spirit

remains at one with the soul of the poet. The Maximin experience from now on colors all Stefan George's work. The mission of the poet is shown in *Der Stern des Bundes* (1914). His task is to draw young men to himself and teach them the will of God: that is, the law of a new life, described in George's last volume, *Das neue Reich* (1928). The principles on which this life is based are complete self-discipline, acceptance of fate, veneration of the Leader. When these young men become mature, they will in turn be leaders.

A circle of gifted young men surrounded the poet at Darmstadt—the much-discussed and much-ridiculed *Kreis*. Some of these disciples, unable to bear the atmosphere of worship around the elder man, broke away, followed by the master's measured thunder.

It is too early yet to gauge the actual influence of Stefan George on German literature. His style displays a most exacting workmanship. Not merely rhyme and rhythm but the sequence of vowels and consonants in each line and poem of his mature years are deliberately calculated for effect. The doctrines expressed show a striking resemblance to National Socialist ways of thinking, but George's ideas really rest on a different foundation; where National Socialism wants power for the sake of power, George calls for utter selflessness, and devotion of the leader to his flock. His poems are referred to with great admiration in present-day Germany, though hardly anyone reads them.

The other poet of genius, Rainer Maria Rilke, stands alone. He knows only one reality: God. At first his devotion is emotional, and his early poems, much beloved by the young postwar generation, dissolve in soft color and sound. His outer life runs an uneventful course, and the sensitive artist feels the impact of this

everyday life and fears that the duties of Everyman will
kill his creative genius. *Ich bin zuhause zwischen Tag und
Traum*—"I am at home between the day and the dream"
—this early line shows him shrinking from the "day,"
which to him symbolizes action and the striving for
material ends, and seems typical of his attitude toward
the common lot of man at the time.

A change came with his trip to Russia in 1900. The
mystic element in Russian worship struck a chord in his
soul which never ceased to vibrate. "That Russia is my
home is a part of the great and mysterious security from
which my life springs," he writes in 1904 from Rome.
Das Stundenbuch (1899–1903) is the fruit of this ex-
perience; here his devotion has deepened and broadened,
and he finds in God the pervasive element of all life.

His friendship with Rodin in Paris, formed in 1906,
marked a new phase. From the great sculptor he learned
the ideal of untiring work, of order, and severe form. A
deep feeling of responsibility was born in him. He came
to know that he could not serve humanity by living
withdrawn, like a monk, but only by living as a human
being among other humans, where, as he put it, the day
is realized in simplicity. *Die neuen Gedichte* (1907 and
1908) belong to this period. He married Clara Westhoff,
sculptor and painter of the Worpswede school, and they
had a daughter. But the necessity of living for his art, of
conserving for it every atom of strength in his frail body,
separated him from his family, though he stayed on
terms of friendship with them. His last years were spent
in the small mountain castle of Muzot in Switzerland.
His final conception of the world and of life is given in
Sonette an Orpheus (1923) and in the *Duineser Elegien*,
begun in 1912 and finished in 1923. Through profound
symbols, although in simple language, he conveys his

experience of reality: that the world as we know it is becoming more and more meaningless, and our only salvation lies in man's capacity to build a new and valid world in his own soul.

This is, in bare outline, the inheritance left by these two gifted men. It will be our task to see how three poets now living deal with what they have received from the past, and how their work reflects the reality around them. In the case of Weinheber and Steffen we shall analyze only their poems, since their prose work shows no lyric traits. But as Carossa's novels have a lyric character and are recognized as largely autobiographic, they will be considered together with his poetic output.

HANS CAROSSA

TO approach the poet Carossa with the coolly avowed purpose of analyzing his concept of reality seems like an impertinence. The excuse must be that, at a time when all values are being reconsidered, it is important to discover the relation of outstanding personalities to the world around them.

Carossa was born in 1878 in Tölz, a Bavarian watering place; later the family moved to other little towns. His father was a country doctor. His mother, a devout Catholic, was occasionally haunted by feelings of sinfulness and an ensuing apprehension of danger. At such times she taught the boy to imitate the lives of the saints—to give away his toys and walk barefoot in atonement of sin. Always inclined toward exaggeration, the child took to inflicting small wounds on himself by pricking his cheeks with pointed leaves of an oleander. The father, thinking this went too far, cured his son by an object lesson. When a patient came with a badly burned arm, the doctor said to Hans:[10] "I see you like to sacrifice yourself. Now show that you are in earnest!" And before the boy knew what was happening, the physician had drawn back the sleeve of his little coat and was taking off particles of skin which he applied to his patient's arm. Young Carossa, frightened at first, stood the test well, and never again resorted to the leaves of the oleander.

When he was about ten years old he was sent to boarding school. Both his early childhood and his years in this Catholic institution are described with inimitable charm in the autobiographical *Kindheit und Jugend*, published in 1922, but written for the most part during the poet's active service in the World War. His boarding-school days came to a strange end; the events leading to his dismissal suggest Carossa's feeling toward poetry as well as his own subconscious development.

On the occasion of a carnival party he became aware for the first time of a younger boy, whose unusual beauty was enhanced by a page's costume. The imagination of young Carossa was captivated at once. He experienced one of those rare moments, unforgettable and deeply our own, when beauty stands before us and in a flash too short and too brilliant to be clearly understood we seem to comprehend the innermost meaning of life. For Carossa this meeting marked the boundary between childhood and adolescence, and the pure flame of spiritual passion enveloped the boy. He wrote a childish poem to his idol, and having lost it in the turmoil of the party, got up at night to look for it. As he wandered around in the dormitory he was found by one of the teachers, a zealous young chaplain who immediately suspected the worst, for it was known that the handsome boy, a young count, was involved in forbidden relations with one of the older pupils. Carossa, subjected to a queer kind of cross examination, finally confessed to misbehavior without understanding in the least what his examiner was talking about. Strangely enough, the little count also "confessed" to relations with young Carossa, probably in order to shield his real friend. Many months later when the ill-starred child was dying of scarlet fever he exonerated Carossa, who had been quietly sent home without being made to realize that he had been expelled.

It was after his own confession, on the night before he was called to the director to be sent away on a "holiday," that Carossa had one of his significant dreams." Since dreams recur frequently in both the life and the work of the mature artist, it will be not uninteresting to examine one of his childhood experiences which he retained in some detail. Carossa himself firmly believed that the pattern of a life, unrecognized by the mind, may reveal itself in dreams.

In this instance he seemed to be doing gymnastics at the horizontal bar, accomplishing the most difficult feats with ease. Suddenly he realized that for years he had not gone to an examination, and went to look for his teacher. Neither sad nor gay, he walked through dimly lit halls. Someone followed and he knew it was the young count, who finally passed him. Carossa lightly pulled the boy's ear, and to his horror it came off in his hand; his little friend ran away, and Carossa knew he would denounce him, but felt no particular fear. However, it seemed important that he should follow the child to put back the ear, which was beginning to bother him. In a classroom he found his mother, bending over the little count and sewing down his eyelids with gray silk; the child looked serenely happy. Carossa, quite unimpressed by the scene, ran to find the chaplain, who began to change, first into the director of the school, then into Goethe, whose picture Carossa had recently seen. "Here is the innocent ear," Carossa wanted to say but was unable to speak. Goethe seemed impatient, his fingers drummed on the desk, and a thundering train entered the hall of a church. "Your poem?" said Goethe.

At this moment the boy understood that the poet was on the point of departure. Instead of an ear, his hand now held a sheet of paper covered with indistinct writing. He gave it to Goethe. "We will look at it through the stone Latauge." And as the great man did so, little objects seemed to sprout from the coarse gray paper:

tiny light green leaves, a little branch on which green acorns and red mountain-ash berries grew.

Suddenly a silvery wing came through the paper, and a tiny bird followed. "Good," said Goethe, and wrote a large mark 2 in the margin. Then he looked again at the bird, not larger than a bee, which flew out of the window.

The vivid images in this fantasy reflect the boy's life at the moment, throwing an emphasis on its happenings and people that might not have occurred to his waking mind. His friendship with the little count, that had seemed so important, is overbalanced by the figure of Goethe, who looms large and becomes the judge of the boy's youthful poem. An endearing feature is the modest mark 2, that is, about B or 80%. The importance which poetry has assumed in his subconscious mind is brought out very clearly, as well as an early awareness of Goethe; this was to be a long-continued reverence in his life.

There is indeed a distinct spiritual kinship between the great master of German literature and Carossa. It may be said that the modern poet's life follows the very path outlined for Goethe's Wilhelm Meister who, after a period of striving for general broad education, concluded that specialization rather than a wide range of culture should be the aim of a useful member of society, and became a surgeon. Carossa, son of a country doctor, followed in the steps of his father and it was by this path that he came into contact with the realities of the world. From his father he inherited a high sense of dedication to his profession, not unmixed with a sensitive approach suggestive of poetry rather than medicine. In point of fact, to the elder Carossa also the work of a physician was akin to that of artists and poets. He sometimes disregarded all rational prognosis and treated moribund patients as though they could be healed. Such gentle obstinacy, his son says, is characteristic of physicians who heal by the dictates of their innermost nature rather than by what they learn from books.

The doctor's son realized early that he would not be able to devote his life to poetry—tradition and financial necessity led him to his father's profession. His career was interrupted by the first World War, but his efforts at a clear orientation in life soon become evident. In *Führung und Geleit*, published in 1933, we find a passage dealing with the time when Carossa came back from active service in 1918. Here we see an attempt to maintain an orderly balance between the man of science and the artist. He knows that, returning from the war, he will sit again at sick beds. Often his nights will be interrupted. In the time he can spare from writing the history of others' suffering he may write a few verses or a page of prose. Before the war the narrowness of his life had often depressed him. Now he has come to a place where it is no longer depressing. "Life never flows back to the same channels," he says, and realizes that his profession will not be the same to him as before. He had often in the past wished for an exceptional form of life, believing that his art might be the richer for it. Now he sees that his writing itself will be better if he submits to the common fate of man. He has a feeling for the magic of words, which sway men to evil or to good, and he wants to deal with language as he deals with the healing poisons which he carefully dispenses. Such is the life that he sees before him. "But at the same time I felt clearly that something in my nature contradicted this smug plan; for what, in the end, do we know about ourselves?"[12]

Though he ends his neat scheme of life with a

question mark, Carossa was in a better position than most men to know himself. When he uttered these words he had already written an autobiography, *Kindheit und Jugend* (1922–28) and a war diary, *Rumänisches Tagebuch* (1924), and was just then engaged in setting down a reverential appreciation of the fellow beings who had influenced him.

Moreover, his novels are also to a great extent deliberately autobiographical; he says in fact that autobiography is to him the only means of understanding the common fate of man. He senses that his writing will always be subjective, while his professional life grows more and more objective. As a young physician Carossa was apt to become emotionally involved in the lives of his patients; he is aware of this and proposes to overcome it but realizes that his writing will always be intensely personal.

This parallels the wisdom of Goethe's mature years, and for Carossa also it comes at the end of a long development. We do not discern it, for example, in his first novel, *Doktor Bürger* (1913).[13] The hero of this story, a young physician, identifies himself with his patients to such an extent that life becomes impossible for him, and he ends in suicide. It is a rather confused and badly constructed youthful work but gives an excellent picture of the problems and difficulties of the sensitive doctor-poet.

While reality is too much for Dr. Bürger, in Carossa's second novel *Der Arzt Gion* (1931)[14] the central figure comes to terms with his life and surroundings. Like Bürger, Gion is deeply interested in a young woman who is his patient. But while the pallid heroine of the first novel dies and draws her lover with her, the sculptress Cynthia is a fundamentally healthy person who responds to Gion's treatment. He finally marries the girl, not so much because he is really in love as because he thinks he can help her to find a redeeming balance between art and life. Parallel to this plot runs a second: the fate of a pregnant peasant girl who knows that to bear her illegitimate child will mean death to her frail body, but chooses to give up her life for that of the child. Her ultimate and exalted faith in life for its own sake, and in a future that cannot be fathomed, has a profound influence on the sophisticated people around her, subtly changing the course of their lives. Gion realizes the value of both Cynthia, the artist, and Emerenz, the patient mother-to-be, each in her own sphere, and the bearing of their experience on the destiny of mankind.

His own part in the pattern of their lives is set forth in a central symbol. The spiritual existence of an active man, he thinks, is like that of a besieged fortress. The greater the number of these fortresses, the better it will be for all humanity. They may not know each other, but the holy spirit of mankind knows them and uses them at will. In Gion's feeling, Cynthia and Emerenz, being part of his life, belong to the fortress he must defend. If Cynthia were to succumb to the forces of darkness which threaten her, one of the main fortifications would be lost. She cannot of her own strength overcome her morbid will to isolation, but he feels that he can help her. "She must be preserved, and it is essential that I keep myself so strong, so pure, that I can bind her without clouding her secret crystal. People speak of the marriage of angels and say that it easily turns into a marriage of devils; but perhaps one would have to try such a marriage with her until she awakens to human emotion. And Emerenz is one in a thousand; full of good will and of good faith she wants to bear a child of man to the world.''[15] To their little number he would like to add a young boy, whom he finds in Toni, the waif who operates a telescope in the streets of Munich.

The pattern that Carossa established here is carried through: in the end we see the main characters, Gion, Cynthia, Toni, and the child Johanna whose birth has brought death to Emerenz, all in a balanced relationship which allows each individual his own sphere of freedom. The last pages of the novel are given over to a minor character, a man deranged by the events of the World War and restored to partial sanity by Gion. He is portrayed operating the telescope once owned by Toni—which in the days of his derangement he had regarded as a weapon trained on the sun. He has not, however, regained complete grasp of the realities of ordinary life. Peacefully he stands at the street corner and tells his visions to chosen customers. Nobody takes offense at his fantasies; they only smile and listen with wide eyes when in his muted, feverish voice he tells them what he alone can see: "the center of the sun radiant with youthful spirits, the incantations of the Powers preparing the last war of terrestrial forces, the incandescent chorus of cosmic performers who throw their balls of light millions of times every hour, and have to catch them again without missing a single one, so that the Kingdom of Power and Love at last may come to us."[16]

The novel ends on this surprising note. There is a hint here of an attitude that also appears, more or less veiled, in Carossa's poems, and of which there are traces in his other prose works—that of a dreamlike awareness of cosmic forces, the efforts of which "to bring the Kingdom in" run parallel to those of human beings. But here there is apparently no connection between the two realms, and the cosmic vision is relegated to the mumblings of a deranged man.

A similar undercurrent runs through his latest novel, *Geheimnisse des reifen Lebens*.[17] The story lacks the distinct pattern of the earlier work. The theme is unusual and may well strike the reader as preposterous or even repulsive. Here a man past middle age, married to a semi-invalid, gives a child to a self-sufficient young heiress, who does not wish to submit to the ties of marriage but desires a direct heir to whom she can pass on her inheritance. And such are the delicacy and skill of the author that we follow the experience of his characters without being dismayed by the impossible plot. The main issue here is not so much what actually happens as the portrayal of human beings who strive to evolve a conscious understanding of their experience and inter-relationships. The various degrees of clarity they reach in this appraisal of the reality of their lives become more important to the reader than what they actually do.

The two active characters, Angermann and the young heiress, appear to draw a kind of spiritual sustenance from two unworldly women; these two in turn depend on the worldlings for their physical needs. The heiress Barbara is utterly devoted to a friend who shares her lonely mountain home. Angermann finds himself some-times tormented with jealousy for fear he cannot mean as much to her as the friend, Sibylle. Before living with Barbara, Sibylle herself has found life unbearable and has hovered on the brink of suicide without being able to discern why she feels the overpowering desire to end her life. Staying with the younger rich girl and devoting herself to the care of animals, she finally gets well; "her recovery she owed to Barbara's energetic help, also, though she hardly dared to confess it, to the animals.

Every creature to which she had devoted herself had taken an old load from her soul.''[18]

Angermann's wife Cordula, the other passive character, is even stranger. While Sibylle dresses in rough tweeds and likes to ride horseback, Cordula stays at home, clad preferably in a red silk kimono, smoking innumerable cigarettes and leaving a trail of ashes wherever she goes. On the rare occasions when she leaves the house she is apt to throw a tweed cape over her kimono and face the village unconcerned as to the impression she makes. Oddly enough, the simple people meet her with a kind of reverence, and she is the best friend of all the village children for whom she knits mittens and caps; although they admire even more the fairylike patterns she cuts for them out of colored paper. Angermann regards his wife with a faint distaste, and her familiarity with books on occultism does not make her more attractive to him.

This bare outline does not do justice to the tenderness and delicacy of Carossa's novels; neither plot nor characterization is his forte. The charm of the stories lies in the sensitive descriptions and the long conversations and meditations in which the characters lay bare every fold of their souls; in which also the poet's thoughts are shown, searching—hesitant—but with sudden flashes of insight. A strong tendency toward the spiritual runs through all his works. We often see him groping for extrasensual experiences, and he suffers from a profound dualism which is never quite resolved.

In none of Carossa's novels is the hero moved to action by passion; rather he follows a kind of constructive reasoning. A philosophy born of doubt and weariness is set off against actions intended to serve future life. It seems necessary for life to go on, even though no reason for continuing is given.

The main impression we get from the prose works of Carossa is of an overwhelming sense of responsibility, indeed, a feeling of dedication which at times threatens to engulf the individual. Thus Dr. Bürger becomes the victim of too strong an identification with his patients, and Gion forgets himself to a point where he seems to be merely a member of a group, of a constellation of people, rather than a character in his own right. While Bürger is devoted to individuals, the case is different for Gion and Angermann: they feel themselves responsible to the future. Gion distinctly has the future of mankind at heart. His "fortresses" are to protect and preserve spiritual values in a world that has become inimical to them. They must be handed on to a future race, which will again live by them. Angermann wants continuity of tradition and inheritance, and feels validity in Barbara's wish to pass on her earthly goods to one of her own blood. This, again, is to him a way of preserving the values of the present for an unpredictable future.

Curiously, Angermann himself cannot come to any conclusion as to the nature of these values and consequently does not evolve any definite philosophy of life. Barbara's naïve and unquestioning vitality, in contrast to his own doubting attitudes, seems to him proof that life is intrinsically valuable; although no rational explanation can be found for the desire of human beings to exist. The same phenomenon strikes us here as earlier in the story of Gion: we do not learn what are the actual values to be preserved, and both Gion and Angermann, doubtful of the present, live by a somewhat vague hope for the future.

In *Geheimnisse des reifen Lebens* Angermann says of Sibylle: "Her goal is similar to that which was mine for many years: the vanquishing of death by despising life, complete freedom of the soul, a water-clear existence untouched by fate.''[19] Here is some hint of the Catholic influences brought to bear on Carossa's childhood by his mother and through his school environment. And in his autobiography he tells of his own attempts in this direction.

When he was sixteen years old he suddenly realized that he was, after all, destined to become a saint. He had read in a book on contemplation that there is no better means of sharpening the faculties of the spirit than hunger and silence. ". . . yea, even as a bitter almond-tree may be changed into a sweet one by drawing out part of its sap, so to the fasting one would come visions and ecstasies of which a well-fed person could not even dream.''[20] Attracted by the prospect, the young neophyte embarked on his voyage toward holiness, turning down second helpings at table and doing without in-between snacks, while maintaining a dignified silence when questioned by his contemporaries. They soon found him out, however, and temptation beset the path of the budding saint. He was offered the choicest morsels at table, and presently invited for a special treat: beer and hazelnut cake. The sight of these ill-assorted dainties was too much for his asceticism; he succumbed to gluttony, and that was the end of his youthful attempt to reach "a water-clear existence untouched by fate."

Later, in more mature vein, Carossa turned from mysticism by an act of will. We see his reasoning reflected in the words of Angermann: "Did I ever preach the doctrine of patient contemplation? I do not think that I approve of it any more. Would it be of any help to me, would I become a different person, if suddenly in the darkness of my soul the bright images of all creatures were to confront me? Perhaps it is not our lot at all to gain immediate knowledge of things now hidden, and perhaps we should follow the faithful who only contemplate these things through the medium of a redeemer's crystal heart. Or is there another way for us who do not follow the common path—are there exaltations of the soul, unsought, which grant in a flash that which the patient labor of years does not attain?"[21]

This thought comes to Carossa time and again, and he offers it under many images. He will see, for instance, small blue butterflies quenching their thirst in the faint moisture of the soil near a broad stream; if they were to drink from the stream itself they would be destroyed. "Many people feel a danger of this kind when confronted with the great spiritual elements. They keep away from them and make every effort to cover them all their lives with a layer of forgetfulness, just as we preserve phosphorus under water to save us from a conflagration."[22]

A possible way to reach knowledge of these "great spiritual elements," constituting perhaps the ineffable reality behind phenomena, is suggested to him by his contact with Rainer Maria Rilke. "He [Rilke] said that he had learned from Rodin to look so often and so searchingly at a tree, an animal, a statue, a human being, or a traditional figure of history, that finally an essential vision of the contemplated form emerged in himself. This procedure was not quite unknown to me; a short anthroposophical essay which I happened to read told me the same thing. But I considered such spiritual exercises much too difficult and too time-consuming to attempt them for myself."[23]

He never ceases to hope that such an essential experience of reality will some day be his, even without conscious effort, and especially believes that this may come to pass when he is very old. Then, perhaps, he may reach a state akin to the rare minutes of the evening, when a star already rises in the east while the sun has not quite disappeared—then a higher vision may be attained, surpassing human understanding.[24]

His attitude toward spiritual realization is again parallel to that of Goethe, who also overcame a leaning toward the occult, turning from it by conscious effort during the time of his maturity but admitting that in our old age we all become mystics.

In spite of his emphatic denial of the desirability of reaching knowledge of higher spheres while still in this life, Carossa's poetic work shows instances in which an awareness of a transcending life breaks through his carefully preserved earthly realism. A preoccupation with spiritual spheres of being seems to crowd into his consciousness. A striking example is offered in "Der alte Taschenspieler," a dramatized poem of some length. Here an old magician is talking to his beloved little granddaughter after a successful performance. She often assists him, and now as always she is enraptured by his parlor tricks—the plant that grows before the eyes of the audience, white pigeons flying up to the stars. Though she knows how it is done, her wonder and surprise are ever new. She reminds her grandfather that many years earlier he had done gruesome things, hypnotizing members of the audience and transmitting to them unpleasant experiences. He confesses that in his youth he was given to practices even more dangerous: he was able to fathom the dark subconscious depth of human nature and to use its forces in forbidden ways. India taught him that black magic, and he knows that demons have their part in it. Now, for the sake of his grandchild, he has become a harmless parlor magician.

In another poem, "Das Mädchen von Dobrowlany" (1925), Carossa's preoccupation with occult practices takes the form of a letter to a friend who has "left the clear daylight to which we are born" in order to reach the universe of the spirit (*das Geister-All*) by strict and silent discipline. Carossa says that he does not hope to dissuade his friend from his quest nor does he doubt the validity of his aims. He reminds him, however, of a strange and touching episode they witnessed together during the war: In the fields near a sacked Rumanian village many dead were lying. The friends were surveying this scene of desolation when they saw a girl approach from the flaming village, her hair the color of wheat under a scarlet kerchief. She carried a load of linen and with incredible swiftness undressed one corpse after the other, friends and enemies alike, and shrouded them gently in her linen sheets. Then she sat down, facing them, and seemed to wait quietly for more dead. The friends understood that she was insane, totally oblivious to the danger around her.

Carossa suggests that if we were strong enough to approach the living with the self-forgetting love that this transfigured child gave to the dead, we would be rich enough in our own world and have no need to spy into "the sphere of pale spirits."

Carossa's lyrics show his deliberate love of the earth, to which he turns with fervor:

> Und nur lieber wird uns die Erde
> Wenn sich der Himmel vor ihr verhüllt—*

*And the earth will be the dearer
If the sky has veiled its face.

Gesammelte Gedichte, p. 66.

Wären wir nicht reich genug
In unsrer Welt?
Was hilft's, in andere zu spähn?*

To the eternal values of earth he gives symbolic form in several poems. In "Heimliche Landschaft" (Secret Landscape) a silvery gray snake lies dead and broken in the dust. Children, kneeling down, cover the body with walnut leaves. Hard black beetles come up from the ground to carry back the dead body into the "warm circle of living things."

In "Die Nebel" fog and clouds change to rain and bless the fields below. Another *perpetuum mobile* is shown in "Die Ahnfrau."

Wage dich wieder hervor
Silbernes Mittagsgesicht!
Alle sind aussen im Korn
Alles ist, wie es war.

. . . .

Husch in dein Sterbegemach
Denk nicht vermoderter Pein!
Sieh, wo du seufzend vergingst,
Atmet das blühende Kind.

. . . .

Umfliess es mit Geisterglück!
Nun öffnet es Augen voll Traum.
Es blinzelt durch dich in den Tag;
Es lächelt und schläft wieder ein.

Grüsse die Natter im Flur!
Noch reicht man den Milchnapf ihr fromm.
Dort schleicht sie gesättigt hinaus;
Sie fühlt und fürchtet dich.

*Would we not be rich enough in our world?
What use to spy into another world?

Gesammelte Gedichte, p. 107.

Klug folgt sie verborgener Spur
Hinab in ihr dunkles Gebiet.
Da liegt unter höhligem Stein
Der Schatz, den du vergrubst.

Du sahst in die ferne Zeit.
Du wahrsagtest Krieg und Verfall.
Treu hast du gedarbt und bewahrt.
Die Schlange weiss darum.

Sie hegt auf dem Hort ihre Brut.
Sie biegt sich um ihn jede Nacht
Zum zauberverstärkenden Ring.
Oft klirrt unbändig das Gold.*

    Venture again to approach,
    Silvery vision of noon!
    They are all out in the corn,
    Everything is as it was.

    . . . . . .

    Quick to the room where you died!
    Think not of pain that is dead!
    Lo! Where you sighing expired
    Breathes now a rosy child.

    . . . . . .

    Let your bliss flow around him!
    Now he opens his eyes, full of dreams.
    He gazes through you at the day;
    Sinks again into sleep with a smile.

    Greet now the snake by the door!
    They pour her milk as of old.
    She drinks it and now she glides out;
    She knows you and fears you still.

*Ibid., p. 98. The title of this poem is impossible to translate exactly. "Forefather" would have the right sense and atmosphere, if it occurred in a feminine form.

She follows the secret path
Down to her gloomy den,
Where lies in the hollow stone
The treasure you buried there.

You looked into distant time,
You saw the war and decay.
Faithful, you starved and saved.
The serpent is aware.

She keeps her brood on the hoard.
She coils herself every night
Around it, a magical ring.
The restless gold resounds.

The poet shows us three aspects of an eternal cycle of life: the body of the dead snake is converted to new animal life, the waters connect the elements with the growth of plant life and, on a different plane, the stream of life flows mysteriously through the generations. All these cycles stay within the boundaries of material being to which he clings. They appear to establish for him a certain balance between material and spiritual values, with which he is resolved to be satisfied.

Nevertheless, he does see another possibility: that of, let us say, metamorphosis—an experience repeating itself as it were in a different sphere and with an altered significance. This "metamorphosis" may well be called the deepest experience of Goethe, and one that permeates all his works. It is also a deep and spontaneous part of Carossa's philosophy. Even in his early poems we see traces of it. "Die Flucht," which belongs to the period of *Doktor Bürger*, describes a young physician harassed by the terrible confidence of his dying patients and suddenly seized by the vision of a child in agony. From

the depth of this horror he gleans the hope that the cry
of pain caused by mortal anguish may be a shout of joy
in the universe of the spirit. If this realization is rather
naïve, even crude, in its expression, we will find subtler
forms for similar experiences later. In "Von Lust zu
Lust" (1918) we see the transfiguration of earthly
passion into essential creative forces. "Mysterium der
Liebe" (1919) has the same basic theme: the deadly
danger of human passion and the courage of human
beings who brave these dangers and by overcoming the
sheer power of sex make it possible for Eros to be
incarnated and resurrected in their purified love. These
poems show the persistent idea of sublimation. A re-
currence of the cyclic development, coupled with the
motif of sublimation, appears in the mystic poem,
"Geheimnisse" (1918): A star must consume itself so
that life may flower on earth—and the human being
must reach a stage where he will sacrifice himself and
be consumed in burning service.

In the eternal cycles of life on earth, in the deliberate
effort of the old magician to keep his feet on the ground,
and in the idea of earthly sublimation rather than
spiritual realization, we see Carossa's conscious pursuit
of a normal reality: he would keep away from everything
that distracts his attention from the visible, tangible
world, forgetting the cosmic visions which haunt him.

But let us look more closely at the things of earth to
which this poet clings with such fervor. Nine of the
seventy poems that fill his single slender volume,
Gesammelte Gedichte, treat of morning, noon, and sun,
of a warm joyous existence; but twenty-three poems
have a background of night, fog, or dusk. Often he
cannot face the direct aspect of the sun or the moon;

their reflection in the water has an immediate actualness which satisfies him.

This shifting of the stimulus of his experience has a parallel in his novels. We see it in one of the most charming episodes of his autobiography, in Part II, *Verwandlungen einer Jugend*. By way of punishment for a number of increasingly grave youthful pranks, the boy was locked into an empty classroom to do some extra work. The shock of this solitary confinement proved a turning point—his behavior improved afterwards. During his stay in this classroom he gazed admiringly at a blue map of the constellations which adorned the wall. "Strange; often he had looked up to the sky, by day and by night, but never had the immeasurable quality taken hold of his feelings as it did now when he looked at the artificial planes dotted with stars and foreign signs."[25] It seems to the boy that his soul is so filled with wonder that it expands beyond its capacity and makes room for new experiences. Here again, as in the poetic instances of reflected sunlight, we see the tendency to get from a small concrete thing the impetus of feeling which others might derive from what is in reality vast or brilliant.

Thus in one of the poems on reflections we see him flee the strength of the sun and turn to its pallid image in the water, which he can scatter at will. It is interesting to compare this attitude with that of Faust in the second part of Goethe's drama. Faust faces the rising sun and, unable to bear its overwhelming light, turns from it to contemplate a rainbow forming in a waterfall:

> Dem sinne nach, und du erkennst genauer:
> Am farbigen Abglanz haben wir das Leben. . . .*

---

*"Let your thought dwell upon this, and you will become convinced that in the colored reflection we have life itself." Goethe, *Faust II*, Act I.

he says. This idea is closely connected with that of
revulsion from the supernatural. All through the first
part of the drama he has sought immediate knowledge
of a spiritual world, invoking to that end the help of the
devil. Now he realizes that only the loving contempla-
tion of physical reality on earth will yield the experiences
of spiritual truth. We have seen that Carossa, like
Faust, is drawn toward direct spiritual experience in his
youth, only to turn from it later in favor of what he feels
to be a natural and wholesome spiritual development
through the validating experiences of earth. The parallel
is oddly complete in the quality of Carossa's own re-
actions to the concrete world: his love—precisely—of
reflected things.

And yet by this very element his poems show that he
does not feel altogether at home on earth. In spite of the
consciously optimistic philosophy, we have seen that a
background of dusk prevails in his lyrics. In turning from
the "image" to earthly reality, the brightness of the
world is softened for him. Reflections attract him. Also
clouds—that changing, floating world—are a frequent
component of his landscapes. He shows us "a pale cloud,
its rim dissolved in green; clouds, heavy as sponges
saturated with light; great marble clouds; cloudbanks
pressing down heavily; clouds reflected in water—grey
with deep incisions like oak leaves, having a lining of
blue light; the narrow moon cuts with pale incisiveness
through grey clouds shot with yellow; clouds beginning
to glow, dissolving in a purple haze to let the sun break
through, like a trembling drop of clearest light; a black
storm cloud is shattered into white fragments by a rock
—the landscape is mottled by quick shadows of clouds."

This floating world is in keeping with his love for
images reflected in the water. The feeling of unreality

created here becomes even stronger when we examine the human beings he describes. There are not many of them, and when they do appear the poet is more concerned with their inner experience than with their appearance. We see:

"—a pale girl; a pale barefoot girl in a grey dress; a grey wanderer; a wife, pale in the pallid lamplight, her hair loosened with dreams as with dew; a child flitting like a ghost; an expectant mother looking out into the misty evening where fallen leaves whirl in black waters, her small tired hands resting in her lap; a motherly face pale as a young girl's; the apparition of a dying child; the imagination of a sick boy sees the women who bring the fever:

> Sie scheinen zu lächeln von fern.
> Doch wenn sie näher schleichen,
> Dann sehen sie ganz wie die Toten aus.
> Ihre Augen sind ohne Blick.*

The dream of a dying child: black men scurry around him, the walls float like fog, King and Queen come out of it with crowns—outside snow-white riders with fiery whips wait on dark horses."[26]

This is surely an eerie crowd! The only people permitted to wear brighter colors are certain figures of the poet's memory: a red-cheeked chubby young man and a white-faced tall girl in a green dress—but both reveal to the practiced eye of the doctor that they are marked by death. A girl with hair as light as wheat wears a red kerchief. She is, however, sweetly insane (lest the

---

*They seem to smile from afar.
  But as they creep nearer and nearer,
  They look just as dead people look;
  Their eyes are without sight.

Gesammelte Gedichte, p. 45.

reader be misled into untimely gaiety by her cheerful appearance). Four of his poems are devoted to unborn children—a sign that the unknown future is full of suggestion for him.

The world of Carossa's lyrics is like a landscape in a luminous mist. Sometimes a slanting ray of light reveals the tantalizing outline of a mountain range, or in the valley the dim course of a great river. In the milky silence, shapeless gray figures approach and recede; we do not know whether their gestures are friendly or threatening, whether this floating scene is one of creation or of dissolution.

There are other minor themes and descriptions, many of them of great charm. Carossa is attracted by the world of plants and of animals, though these themes are not more prevalent than with other lyric poets. His choice is interesting: seeds have a peculiar fascination for him; he shows us darting, airy creatures like butter-flies and dragonflies; then again, animals which might play a part in fairy tales or myths: doves, an eagle, a hawk, cats, snakes—these are not dangerous but rather wise or sacred; they live their lives uninfluenced by the world of men.

The metaphors which the poet uses, sparingly and with sensitiveness, make for atmosphere rather than symbolic value. There are however some instances of recurring symbols and they are significant: the world of the stars, the sun, the moon, crystals, ice flowers—all serenely following their own laws and throwing into relief the turbulence and uncertainty of our life. They seem to accentuate the poet's longing for a world with-out strife and tearing emotions, and their serenity contrasts with the constantly fluctuating impressions of surrounding reality. But brief description cannot do justice to the delicate, delightful quality, the spirit of gentleness and love that pervades these poems.

In spite of Carossa's valiant philosophical attempt to accept the life on earth, it seems as though the harsher reality of day and human events had never quite reached the deeper regions of his consciousness, from which his lyric poems spring. However, we do find references to current happenings in his novels, especially in *Geheimnisse des reifen Lebens*. We do not see him taking an active part; characteristically, his attitude is shown in a dream.

He sees himself as a banished prince, passing through the streets of his former capital. A detachment of soldiers marches toward him, the band playing. Nearer and nearer a flag flutters in the light of torches. The dreamer knows his duty: he will have to salute it with a prescribed gesture—death would be meted out to anyone who failed in the ordered response. He knows his son is among those marching and longs to see him. But he cannot remember the form of the salute! Frantic, he tries to think of some sort of speech he might make: "Dear contemporaries! Venerable youth of the country," he will say, "I am not worthy to be punished by you. . . ." But before he can utter a word, the flag is passing, followed by a group of shouting and laughing boys and girls. No one has noticed that he failed to salute; no one has even seen him.[27]

Nothing could express more completely the poet's position in the midst of temporary events: he feels himself standing aside, helpless and unnoticed, while the youth of the country surges toward a new goal. His is not the urge of the prophet or of the leader—he abdicates before he is even challenged.

The same feelings are reflected in this novel, in Angermann's relations with a group of small boys. His very first encounter with them is symbolic. He is lying in a mountain meadow, tired after a long walk in the hot sun. As he looks up at the sky, he is startled by a strange phenomenon: the sun is hidden behind a gray cloud, and protruding from its fiery rim, broad black beams shoot far out into the blue. He closes his eyes, then looks again: the terrible rays are darker than before. Finally he discovers the cause of what proves to be an optical illusion: the sun, hidden behind the gray cloud, does send out rays; they are, however, not broad but rather like narrow lines, and their intensity is such that the eye refuses to take it in. What the blinded vision had taken for black was actually the azure lying between the intensely bright lines.

As he recovers from the startling effect of this apparition, Angermann is approached by a group of small boys. The leader is a child not more than eight years old, his knees torn by brambles, his gray eyes over-serious, lighted by feverish sparks. The man is strongly moved; he feels the glowing strength of these young creatures, driving them imperiously toward an uncertain fate. The children want to form a "comradeship"; they need money for uniforms, a drum, and a flag. Angermann longs to give them advice, to point out to them something of which he himself is only half aware. But he is powerless to do so. Instead, he gives them more money than he can afford, or than they expected.[28]

Later he sees his little friends again; he is himself in a rather peculiar situation. Swimming too long in the cold river, he has reached the end of his strength and is on the point of drowning, when the boys march past on the shore dressed in miniature uniforms, proudly displaying

their flag and their drum. They salute him and, trying
to raise his arm in answer, he nearly goes down for the
third time. In spite of his danger he does not give any
sign of distress, feeling that the children would not even
realize his plight. They march on, and he lapses into a
dreamy state of semiconsciousness. "I may well say I
died." But somehow he recovers suddenly and reaches
shore.[29] It is a touching little scene: the mature man,
unwilling to make clear his plight to the young boys
hurrying on their way, feels no bitterness at their lack
of discernment. It seems right to him that the older
generation should go down unheeded.

On three other occasions Angermann sees the boys.
Once he is able to exert some influence over them: they
are hastening toward a place in the woods where blasting
is going on and there is danger. They do not listen to
his warning, but he sidetracks their attention by showing
them a dead bird and asking them to bury it. They dig a
grave with their little daggers, and after the ceremony
it is too late to go on to the dangerous spot.[30] The next
time he gets only a fleeting glimpse of them as they
march to a festival, hurrying as though their being on
time were of the utmost importance. Intent on their
purpose, they pay no attention to a little procession of
girls whom they pass. At the festival he sees them for
the last time as they stand around a bonfire, watching
the streaming red silk of the flames, entranced, as if only
waiting for an order to rush into the fire and immolate
themselves.[31] Looking on, he analyzes his impressions.
His own youth had been sheltered and secure; theirs is
surrounded by constant revolution. Their will is tensed
and they dream battle. Yet his own generation so
peacefully reared was called to war. And what, Anger-
mann asks (in this novel dated 1936), will be the fate of

these young warriors? Will they follow the fierce call to battle? If this should happen, only clear victory or destruction could be the outcome.

But the gentle spirit of Carossa shrinks from this terrible and uncompromising destiny. He sees, instead, the possibility that after the era of the first World War and subsequent revolutionary adjustments, an entirely different age will emerge; a deep self-realization of all nations is perhaps very close, and tasks so great may be imminent that war will have no more room in the scheme of human evolution. Then may dawn a new knowledge of the meaning of life on earth, and the burning courage of these boys will find its goal.

Such are the poet's dreams of the future. But what of the present, beside which such thoughts seem very remote? What of the part a man must play now? Carossa has an answer: "May each one of us preserve deep in himself a cell surrounded by silence! There, from suffering and happiness, may grow the thoughts which are the salt of the future, even if they are never written down!"[32] The children, he goes on to say, must hold to the comradeships they have formed, and harden themselves, waiting patiently for their hour which is sure to come. Then they will come into their own without having to use force; then the youth of the world will have only one common enemy, the spirit of darkness and of lies. They will conquer it, and the generation to which Carossa belongs will rest in peace.

We do not know how the poet feels, now that events must have forced a reconsideration of his stand. He has just published a new book: *Das Jahr der schönen Täuschungen* (Leipzig, 1941)—"The Year of Beautiful Illusions." It is a continuation of his autobiography. As it has not yet reached these shores, it cannot be discussed here. From critical accounts in periodicals still accessible we may infer that his style has not changed, and the subject matter shows him concerned with the past: the book deals with a year of study in Munich, in 1897–98.

As we review the qualities of this gifted poet, certain points emerge. The lack of clear-cut evaluation, of intellectual criticism, so evident in his dealing with the present situation, seems to be with Carossa a basic attitude. Such processes are alien to his personality. He does not merely avoid them; he shrinks from uncompromising clarity here as he shrinks from it in all other aspects, preferring a floating and luminous haze to any merciless light or focus. He is not critical of his contemporaries but enters into their world with fellow feeling, seeing them as human beings no matter what the implications of their actions may be. No doubt his medical profession predisposes him for this—a doctor, complete partisan of life, will do what he can for it, no matter what its guise.

Open criticism of National Socialism was not, of course, possible to Carossa if he was to stay in the country. His reflection of the movement in the incidents of the little boys is, however, quite apparent, although characteristically—and necessarily—veiled. Here his hope for the future is coupled with apprehension of the danger threatening these tense and feverish young creatures. The poet is obviously disturbed; a feeling of uneasiness and doubt is unmistakable. His personal role is brought out in the dream of the flag. From a bleak yet stoical isolation, which clearly hurts the more since it envelops a being warm and sensitive to the life around him, he assures the "venerable youth" of the country that he will not hamper them. He does not feel compelled to take action.

Among the factors that may have contributed to Carossa's political inertia is the fact that his energies must have been partly absorbed by his profession. In German tradition, also, it would be unusual for a medical man to show marked interest in the affairs of the nation. And there is yet another, more sinister possibility: foreigners traveling in Germany just before the outbreak of hostilities have been amazed to find how consistently Germans do not realize, and if told are unable to believe, many things known to have happened in their own country.

But the part of a spectator which Carossa chooses for himself is one that cultivated people have frequently assumed in the decades between the two World Wars. This quiescent attitude is difficult to understand in a vigorous nation where optimism and the will to action are traditional, as in the United States. In central Europe a long series of devastating national experiences has left many people of good will feeling that their energies will be wasted if they try to oppose the powers that sweep nations. It is natural for a European to assume the oblique approach, as it were, following a line of action which, while not directly opposing the destructive current, may yet deflect it in the end.

In the face of such influences we cannot be surprised that a poet refrains from immediate political reaction. Yet it is clear that his energies, far from being apathetic, are focused on a mission for the future. Only that mission is of a different nature from direct action: he has a deep feeling of responsibility toward values of life and growth which must be preserved in a world dark with hate and fear. His poetry and his close searching of life both serve this end. And it is not impossible that a certain wisdom and perspective, incorporated in the little allegories of the novels, are intended one day, by their mild and sympathetic form, to reach minds which have become inaccessible to direct criticism.

The main images which express his attitude of preservation are the recurring "cell" and "fortress." Nothing could show more clearly his subconscious awareness of danger and isolation in an inimical world. There is in them also the constant implication of something enduring, holding out, something to fertilize the future The same deep sense of continuity appears here as in the poet's strong feeling for the cycles of life.

However the cell and the fortress imply another kind of detachment as well: he seems to feel not merely set apart from the material scene around him; his cell suggests a separation also from "cosmic forces" whose efforts to bring in the Kingdom of Power and Love are dimly seen in the episode of the man with the telescope, and whose potential willingness to help is indicated elsewhere, as in Gion's mention of the "Holy Spirit of Mankind" who will eventually use the fortresses for its own ends. These powers are never focused clearly— they are too brilliant and too vast. An all-too-human element comes in here. It will be remembered that he discards with some impatience the procedure that Rilke had learned from Rodin, and which he finds also described in an essay: to look so often and so searchingly at an object that finally an essential vision emerges. Carossa says a little plaintively that such a course, while probably rewarding, is too difficult—and too time-consuming—for him. As in this instance he did not learn from Rilke, so in his style also Carossa went uninfluenced by his beloved friend.

Reading his verses and his lyric prose, we feel in them an element of natural growth, not one of conscious mastery as we see for instance in Stefan George. On the whole, Carossa is curiously untouched by the heritage of the nineteenth and twentieth centuries; his ancestor is Goethe, though his relation to the great master is one of kinship, not of imitation. It is appropriate that the Goethepreis of 1938 was given to Carossa.

In his own right, and in a high sense, Carossa is a poet, and it is as a poet that he seeks to resolve the problems set up by the impact of the total world on the individual. In the ideas of metamorphosis, of sublimation, of sacrifice and responsibility, his poems combine the demands of life on earth with the selfish instincts of man, and assimilate to a certain degree the great spiritual forces from whose immediate experience Carossa shrinks. Thus elements which by themselves would war against each other are blended and made fruitful. Here the poet fulfills the promise he gave himself: to heal with words as the doctor heals. His poignant and moving verses with their deep sympathetic feeling for nature and human life give moments of comfort and glimpses of better possibilities to his harassed contemporaries; although the reader may sometimes feel that his art, with all its gentle radiance, resembles the butterflies who drink from the faint moisture at the river bank lest the great stream should kill them.

It may well be that Carossa's deepest impulses, dimly seen in his past work, will crystallize in the future and reflect more clearly the reality he seeks. In an enigmatic and tantalizing sentence prefacing his war diary, he compresses the essence of his search: *Raube das Licht aus dem Rachen der Schlange*—"Snatch the light from the jaws of the serpent!"

JOSEF WEINHEBER

THE literary figure of Josef Weinheber presents a contrast to Carossa, and his life and background also are as dissimilar to the Bavarian's as though these two men had lived on different planets.

There is nothing in Weinheber's childhood and very little in his adolescence that foreshadows the fastidious artist we see later—rather, one may say, his fastidiousness develops in spite of his sordid surroundings.

Born in 1892 in a village near Vienna, the boy lost his father very early. He always remembered the man's gaiety, his great voice raised in lusty song, his exuberant strength. He was in fact a boisterous butcher, well known for his prowess in drink and love-making. Weinheber's mother died not many years after; her shadowy form, beautiful and silent with heavy dark-brown tresses, glides through her son's lyrics. She as well as two daughters died of tuberculosis. The boy was educated in a charitable institution, where he followed the *gymnasium* course. Here he acquired a mastery of Latin and Greek, and his studies gave him a taste for refinement quite out of reach of a pauper. Outside the classroom life was bleak—he describes it in his first and only novel, *Das Waisenhaus* (1925). A book without beauty, sadly lacking unity and crude in style, it shows a sex-starved adolescent, full of violent and conflicting emotions and ambitions. Weinheber himself would like to forget this novel, and it has long been out of print. Nothing in it shows promise unless it be the drive of an ill-directed vitality.

Before his course of study was completed the boy left the orphanage, penniless. A time of sordid poverty followed; finally he managed to get a position as a postal clerk. He completed his studies in evening school, and now began to write poetry.

For years he was hampered by poverty and embittered by the lack of an appreciative audience. However, his devotion to his calling did not flag, and he continued to write, attaining ultimately a considerable reputation. He still lives in Vienna, apparently in comparative affluence, and recognized as a poet of the Third Reich. But his real home is the "strange world of art, which, far away from the real one, and better than it, exists in spirit. There, lofty names are ranged like shields around a heart left alone: Alkaios and Sappho, Marcus Aurelius and Schopenhauer, Hölderlin and Droste. They are indeed, and more than my city, my indestructible home; more than my fathers, they are my ancestors."[33]

In considering the lyric work of the man, the reader is struck first by his unusual versatility. Weinheber has mastered a vast variety of known and several heretofore unknown forms and meters; his handling of words is intoxicating. He uses with complete ease the intricate pattern of the Greek ode, the measured severity of the sonnet, the sophisticated simplicity of the "Lied," the balanced cadence of free verse. The reader is carried away by splendor of rhythm and colorful interplay of vowels and consonants, by astonishing intricacies of rhyme. All this richness—the witchery of the sensual impact of words—cannot of course be conveyed in another language. It does not concern us here except as an explanation of the poet's success.

His audacity in using poetic forms seems to stop at nothing. Merely to practice scales, as it were, he transforms one of the liquid odes of the romantic poet Hölderlin, whom he worships.[34] He rearranges the words of this ode—the form of which would seem as inevitable as the sequence of notes in the song of a wood thrush—and marshals them in different meters under the headings: transformation into a sapphic strophe; dissolution into dactylic rhythm; variation of content (Speaks a man of this world—The dead man speaks, the man of the other world); reincarnation in time (working separate phrases into independent forms: Notturno, Scherzo, Rondo); forming a new poem from the original word material; transformation into an asclepiadeic-glyconic (fourth asclepiadeic) strophe. This rather uncanny performance is equaled by other *tours de force*. For example, the forty odes of his cycle, *Zwischen Göttern und Dämonen*,[35] are divided into ten parts of four odes each. Weinheber himself compares this arrangement to flights of pillars. Every ode has four verses, measuring four lines or steps each—as the poet tells us, each of these lines may be measured by the duration of four heartbeats. (This is quite accurate by an average pulse.) Not without apprehension, the reader asks: Is this art, or just a series of tricks of agility?

A feat surpassing that of the pillars and heartbeats surprises us in several sonnet cycles. The scheme is transparent enough, and we recommend imitation to anyone wishing to submit to rigorous technical discipline: Write the last one of fifteen sonnets first. Then use its first line to begin the first sonnet of your cycle, the second line to end it and begin sonnet number two. The third line of sonnet fifteen will become the last line of the second sonnet, as well as the first of number three, and so on. This exercise should greatly increase the neophyte's proficiency in use of the sonnet form.

Slightly dazed by so much verbal brilliance, we turn from form to content, in an endeavor to learn what the poet wishes to convey. Our task in discovering his essential meaning is made less difficult by the fact that Weinheber himself has obligingly outlined in prose his concept of reality.

In "Gedanken zu meiner Disziplin"[36] we read: "Man is not set apart from 'dumb' creatures by the fact that he has a mind, but by the mysterious possibility of giving in language body and form to his mind. Only language justifies the claim that man is a higher being. Language is the reality of the spirit, and through it man becomes a spiritual reality." This sounds as though language were an entity quite apart from man, who becomes real only so far as he identifies himself with it. Language here transcends its recognized mission as a means of expression or, at its highest, of communication, and becomes vibrant with a life of its own. Weinheber goes on: "But this reality is not given to mankind as an undivided entity; it is split into idioms. Each idiom expresses that part of humanity which appears as a 'Folk,' and in certain circumstances as a nation. A Folk is a vital reality, and its language *is* its spiritual nature." He goes even further: an actual spiritual being, called by Weinheber *menschheitliches Teilwesen* (approximately: the oversoul of a part of humanity), manifests itself in each idiom.

We see why Weinheber has proved so acceptable to the National Socialist regime: the individual is nothing; only the Folk, expressed in language, is real. But where the current conception is a mere abstraction, the poet imagines actual spiritual beings, whose manifestations in the visible world are distinct parts of humanity, each a Folk or people. The author proceeds: "Language contains and preserves the fate, the past, and every spiritual possession of a Folk. A people does not lose its dignity by the loss of wars, but by the defilement of its language, and the real arch-traitor is the perverter of language. The highest treasure a people possesses . . . has been confided as an object of spiritual value to its poets." Further on he defines the mission of the poet more specifically: in a "young" language there is a mysterious relation between man and the world—words are, by their very sound, the symbols of real things. As an example he gives the word *Mund* (mouth). The initial M, Weinheber says, illustrates the lips compressed in readiness for speech—the syllable "und" brings to mind the image of something dark and hollow—which is also evident in the Latin *os, oris*. In one of his odes[37] Weinheber poetically explains the sensual appeal of vowels and consonants—as poets and serious critics have tried time and again to do: gloomy U reminds us of tombs, but also of velvet June nights. O swings like the tones of a bronze gong; H heals the broken heart by the power of hallowed heights—even though it is only a letter, H is high, the breath of life is in its holy whisper. Wild and angry K commands combat; but God is mild, and lets the L of love follow gently. In this way, language consists primarily in sound-images which a young people creates spontaneously. But the magic relation between language and reality is lost in time by the ever-changing meaning of words—that, Weinheber says, is the Babylonic confusion of tongues.

The student of language will recognize snatches of alluring trends of thought—theories of the origin of language present themselves, and the little-explored complex of "sound image," "sound symbols"—but we must forego here all attempts at tracing the ancestry of Weinheber's ideas.

The true mission of the poet, as Weinheber sees it,

consists in taking over consciously the spontaneous and inspired creation which in a dim past was the function of the Folk.[38] The poet must now infuse new blood into the language by creating sound-images of real things. An old phase of creation has come to an end; the modern role of the poet consists in using his conscious mind, his lucid intelligence, as a substitute for the intuitive forces which performed this function in ancient times. When Weinheber formulates his thoughts in prose, one sees him working toward this new phase; in his actual creative process he often goes back to what by his own definition would be an atavistic method. We find poems clearly indicating an "inspired" rather than intellectual or conscious mode of poetic impulse:

> Du gabst im Schlafe, Gott, mir das Gedicht.
> Ich werde es im Wachen nie begreifen.
>   .   .   .   .
> Da es ein Klang war, sollt' ich es nicht hören?
> Da es ein Bild war, sollt' ich es nicht sehn?*

This is a description of actual composition, not of a forgotten dream as it might appear. Evidently the conscious mind plays a very small part in poetic conception as described here. If Weinheber is aware of any contradiction, he does not tell us so. But the "intuitive" manner of composition is so frequent with him that one feels an essential conflict between his formulated philosophy of art and his mode of creating.

*The poem, God, you gave me in my sleep;
In waking I shall never understand it.
          .   .   .   .
Since it was sound, why shall I never hear it?
It was an image—shall I never see?

Adel und Untergang, p. 74.

A deeper contradiction and source of uneasiness are apparent in the focusing of his mind on the annihilation of the individual in favor of a transcendent being, manifest in the Folk. Yet if the individual is to function intelligently and lucidly, he must preserve his integrity and cannot be wholly submerged. This conflict never seems to become clearly defined in Weinheber's mind but it colors much of his art. The terror that seizes the human being when he feels his individuality threatened comes out in a short poem:

> Der Wind stand still, das Licht, das Licht
> Wie ein weisser Strom übers Wasser sprang.
> Der Baum hielt schaudernd den Atem an,
> Der tote Stein erklang.
> Der See trank alle Dinge in sich,
> Den Mond und den trotzigen Berg.
> In bodenlosen Abgrund versank
> Ein auf den Tod geängsteter Zwerg,
> Mein Ich.*

Here the human ego, seen as a dwarf shrinking in the face of annihilation, recoils in horror. But there is another, and more insidious aspect of self-immolation. Weinheber knows of this, too:

*The wind stood still; the light, the light
  Like a white stream overleapt the lake,
  The tree all shuddering held its breath,
  The cold dead stone gave voice.
  The lake drank in all things around,
  The moon and the stubborn hill.
  The dark and bottomless pit engulfed
  A dwarf trembling in deadliest fear—
  My Self.

Vereinsamtes Herz, p. 34.

Dennoch: ist nicht des Menschen
Glück, sich fallen zu lassen?
Unterm Schauern des Fremden
ganz, und wie in ein Dickicht

Tief und tiefer hineinzu-
gehn ins eigene Fernweh,
Durch das Dämmer hindurch, die
eigne Raubtiergefahr, bis

zu dem heimlichen, kleinen
weissen Tempel im Urwald,
wo—welch Wiedersehn aus den
vielen, früheren Leben—

wo der Gott gross thront mit den
goldnen Augen (nicht grausam,
nur voll Ewigem), der des
Menschen Süssestes löscht: das Denken?*

This poem is one of the cycle, *Zwischen Göttern und Dämonen*, which we must examine presently.

*But then: is it not human
Bliss to let oneself sink down?
Into shuddering strangeness,
Quite, and as into thickets,
Deep and deeper to go
Into one's own secret longing,
Through the gloaming, and through the
Captured beasts in our own breast
To the small secret temple,
White in untrodden jungles
Where the God whom we knew well
In existences long past—
Where the God sits enthronèd
With golden eyes (not cruel,
But full of eternal things), crushing
What is sweetest in humans: the Thinker?

Zwischen Göttern und Dämonen, p. 24.

Weinheber's idea of what is valid reality amounts to this: Transcendent beings find their visible embodiment in the Folk and manifest their own higher reality in the language of different peoples of the earth. The individual is nothing in the face of these beings. As Weinheber has an exalted opinion of the poet's mission, his spontaneous poetic utterances show sometimes terror, sometimes fascination and a self-intoxicated kind of exhilaration when faced with the submergence of the human entity.

The poet's conscious effort to find a philosophy of reality has a counterpart in Rosenberg's *Der Mythus des zwanzigsten Jahrhunderts*, an account of mystical conceptions underlying the National Socialist Weltanschauung. Here we read: "The essence of the world revolution of today lies in the awakening of racial types."[39] "The strongest personality of our day no longer aspires toward personality but toward the type."[40] "Individualism and universalism are . . . philosophies of decadence."[41] "Today we know at last the forces of the racial soul awakening from a deep sleep."[42] All these utterances are death sentences pronounced on the individual, and the poet, half in terror, half in fascination, feels the forces at work.

We have so far touched upon Weinheber's consciously formulated idea of reality. Let us see now how this compares with the attitudes set forth in his cycle of odes, *Zwischen Göttern und Dämonen*, the disciplined form of which we have already mentioned. In his prose analysis he finds in the soul of the race, expressed in the language of a Folk, the only valid reality. One is surprised to see that in his cycle of odes this conception occurs only once, as it were in passing; he discards it immediately. The critic Pongs[43] extolls *Zwischen Göttern und*

Dämonen as an answer to the eternal quest for the mean-
ing of life. Try as I may, I have not been able to see it as
such. The odes seem to consist of a series of groping
attempts to discover a valid reality; a discovery which in
Weinheber's prose analysis is already confidently
announced.

Many possibilities are explored, and a curious my-
thology develops. In ancient times, the poet feels, man
was real—his soul a battling ground for the great
forces of gods and demons. But now the gods have
withdrawn, though to deny their existence would be
utter folly, and would mean death in life. The demons,
once strong and powerful, are now degraded to thin
specters. Having lost the strong reality of these spiritual
powers, man turns to earth but finds it barren. Time and
again Weinheber falls back on the medieval idea of the
sinfulness and unreality of the "world": man may be
saved only by atoning, he tells us darkly, though he fails
to explain for what we should atone, or how. But if we
do, an unspecified reward will come to us in an undefined
higher sphere. The helplessness of this poet in the face
of religious ideology is striking; he gives us simply
shells of ideas, without content. He knows that there
have been human beings for whom these things were
real; the saints, as they are called. Remote from the
demands of earth, the saint goes on his way like a star,
like a distant storm. We do not understand him, but our
admiring love follows him. This, however, will not
make life on earth bearable; we still feel stifled and our
senses, bringing us the beauty of fragrance, color, and
sound, only serve to obscure true reality.

Here speaks the disciple of Kant; a totally different
trend opened up by Goethe has not influenced this poet—
not for him did Goethe write: *Den Sinnen hast du dann*

*zu trauen—Kein Falsches lassen sie dich schauen.** For
Weinheber, the lovely things of the earth, children and
flowers, only intensify the grief caused by the senseless-
ness of everything—the fact that he can find no essential
meaning in life.

Finally, the poet sees duration and reality only in
death. He does know, however, that to many people it is
possible to live naïvely. Perhaps, he thinks, God does
not want us to find truth. Nevertheless the lonely
thinker must go on with his quest. Rather surprisingly,
at this point Weinheber tells us that the solution of all
problems is—love. This idea hangs in thin air, and the
poet leaves it there to explore other possible roads to
ultimate truth. Man, he continues, may find eternity in
woman who will give rest to his endless striving. He
may find it in the preservation of mankind through the
generations. These thoughts are put before us dis-
passionately and without comment. The poet grows
more emotional when he warns those who would extoll
duty as the meaning of life. At best, he says, doing one's
duty can be a crutch on which to limp through the day;
but doing for the sake of doing makes man cruel, and
charity flees from the noise which accomplished duty
spreads around us. The brave man knows only one duty:
to be himself. This sounds like a momentary dawn of
individualism—but it is followed immediately by the
ode already quoted, depicting the complete and volup-
tuous self-surrender of the thinking individual.

Again, he turns to the hope of solving the riddle of
existence by following the great saints, among whom he
classes Christ and Francis of Assisi. It is striking that he

---

*You must then trust to the senses—they will not mislead you. Goethe,
Vermächtnis (Kein Wesen . . .).

sees no essential difference between Christ and the
saints. In certain of his other lyrics we find him exploring
the possibilities of Christian religion. His feeling is
parallel to that of Faust when he says: *Nach jenen
Sphären wag ich nicht zu streben, woher die holde Bot-
schaft tönt.** He does not disbelieve the reality of Christ,
but the "gentle message" is not for him, nor does he feel
that it has any place in life on earth. Angels sing the
distant song of sweet mediation, he says; the soul longs
for salvation, but earth delegates it to the stars; there it
rests in eternal power. He feels terrible forces at work
and sees man sometimes as the horrible lord of the
earth, who speaks of God and crushes his neighbor as he
would crush a flower. But this lord is powerless against
his own inventions and helpless in his flight from terror;
he has only violence as his last resort.

It is constantly evident that the poet is haunted by an
apprehension of senselessness in life. Man is lost on a
terrible sea, only dreaming of distant islands. Still, he
must stand upright and prove his noble courage, even
though he cannot see any goal in life. The world is lost,
the sacrifice of Christ is vain. A poem of pure beauty,
entitled "Corpus Mysticum,"[44] crystallizes these emo-
tions in an unforgettable sequence of images: Toward
evening the white deer, fairy-eyed, steps from God's
forest. Free from desire, it walks through the blue glade
where silvery bells are swinging in the breeze, and the
moon, in her pale beauty, seems to be eternal in the sky.
Distant weeping tells of sin and atonement. But the
paschal creature cannot bring help: "Death is here, and
will always be here. Withdraw your presence from
bread and wine," the poet calls to the mystical deer.

---

*I do not dare to aspire to the spheres whence comes the gentle message.
Goethe, *Faust I.*

In the eighth and ninth sections of *Zwischen Göttern und Dämonen* Weinheber bows to current ideals: the only reality in life is the youth of a nation; not one beautiful youth, such as to the Greeks personified a god, but youth in general, all the young men of a Folk. They alone bring the God, and the God draws them to himself. In the tenth section the poet seems to have forgotten that youth is the only reality, and claiming that man does not live by bread but by the dream, he comes to the conclusion that the beautiful soul of a Folk is its "sacred dark art."

In spite of the undoubted beauty of some odes, the total effect of the cycle is one of bewilderment. There seems to be much ado about very little; the poet, setting out with great pomp, loses himself in a maze. Certain aspects of his meandering are significant: he cannot free himself from dualism, regarding the visible and tangible reality as inferior to a rather obscurely conceived world of the spirit. "Things" seem dead to him. His secret love and longing, one would guess, belong to the urge of self-annihilation, a trend not uncommon in Europe today. Still he is willing to concede much to the gods of the day, in spite of his talk of heroic freedom. His conception of religion is hazy and confined to sentimental and nostalgic reminiscences of Francis of Assisi and Christ: in his scheme of things neither has to do with life on earth; both live in an undefined higher sphere.

Weinheber's symbols reflect the dualism of his Weltanschauung: throughout the cycle we find the contrast between "day" and "night." The value he gives to these symbols changes in the course of the cycle. In the beginning, "day" is an idol; his attributes—fragrance, sound, and color (the attributes of reality)—obscure a

deeper truth. This evidently parallels the East Indian
philosophic idea of *Maja*—the world of fragrance, color,
and sound which is an illusion given to us by our senses
in time and space and hides a deeper reality only dis-
closed to the searching soul. This "deeper reality" for
Weinheber is "dark"—thus he qualifies the things that
mean most to him, language and art. "And the magnifi-
cent dark language goes down to be devoured by the
day." Also "day" is the life of naïve unthinking multi-
tudes: day and small happiness are their only reason for
living. They do not feel the dark urge of those great
ones who know nothing of the day and happiness, and
who leave us when we try to call ourselves their equals.
The demon, enticing them with numbers, subject to
time—these also are traditional attributes of reality—
throws them into temptation; he devours their minds
by day and their hearts by night. Clearly here the life of
endlessly merging and changing worldly appearances is
the attribute of day; dark and powerful emotion that of
night. At night the soul, lost in dreams, calls her faithful
ones. The poet urges all brave men to plunge into the
night. The tangible and outer existence of man some-
times senses night but turns away from it, preferring to
go around and around, fearing that the straight line
leading out of the eternal circle "might be condemned
in the council of the Gods."

In the greater part of the odes "night" stands for the
darkness underlying all life, superior to the common
light in which we have our being. Out of it come the
dreams that govern our actions. There is, however, a
short interlude in which the symbol changes its meaning.
Interestingly enough, this change coincides with the
odes in which Weinheber pays tribute to the gods of the
hour by extolling youth. Suddenly "day" is superior:

youth is like a beautiful bird in the light of day, giving a new symbol to the land. Nobility is dark no more but belongs to things of light. The demons in the house of darkness hide themselves wisely. The older generation, once worthy of high office, goes down, and the dark wing of night rushes over them.

But as soon as the poet's conscious bow to current opinion is made, the old supremacy of the "night" symbol is reëstablished: we hear again of the beautiful dark art, and while the poet hopes that the God of Light will always give us bright nobility, he does feel that purifying darkness will remain our well of impulse. This reversal in the meaning of an established metaphor seems highly significant. In it by conscious effort and for extraneous reasons the poet controverts the dictates of his deeper experience.

Weinheber does not always dwell in these lofty regions. Two volumes show an entirely different side: *Wien wörtlich*, 1935, and *O Mensch gib Acht*, 1937. Here he deliberately assumes the part of a poet "of the people for the people" and says as much in the introductory verses to *Wien wörtlich:* his Viennese countrymen, he hopes, will say that these poems were not written by a Goethe or Schiller, not by a classic poet or genius, but by one of them. They are vignettes of Viennese life and boisterous drinking songs. *O Mensch gib Acht* bears the subtitle: *An Edifying Almanach for City and Countryfolk*. It gives homely advice in a "folksy" style. The two books help to round out the picture of his unusual versatility.

His other volumes have the same atmosphere as *Zwischen Göttern und Dämonen*. Infatuation with the "night" symbol is found especially in *Adel und Untergang*, 1934, and *Späte Krone*, 1936. In the first, "night"

appears often as the dangerous realm into which the
hero plunges to prove his courage. It is the forbidden
sphere of intoxication, of chaos; but there also is born
the impulse to overcome the dark forces. It is durable as
death and as the vanity of things.

In *Späte Krone* we see night as the sanctuary of the
wounded poet. Divinity acts in its healing darkness.
However, youth must not worship night, or her dark
son, Intoxication; he may be divine—but this god is
horrible. There is a sonnet[45] which extolls night by the
hypnotic device of repetition; a single short line, "the
night is great," occurs five times within the fourteen.
The reader feels the line chanted by a multitude, re-
sponding to a priest of darkness who succumbs more and
more to his own rite, finally falling prey to the powers
he worships.

A series of fifteen sonnets is based on the translation
of Michelangelo's sonnet, "O Nott', O dolce tempo
benché nero."[46] The imagery with which Weinheber
invests night in the first of this series reminds us of
Rilke's style in his last elegies. He calls it "dark lake of
fear, mountain range of suffering, landscape with a
glade of sobs and brooks of tears, thicket of vice, swamp
of intoxication." The very accumulation of images makes
it impossible to visualize anything—like the heaped
metaphors of baroque poetry, they crush the subject out
of existence, giving the reader a feeling of unreality.
The cycle ends in complete fatalism: bright Abel will be
slain by dark Cain; the occident is doomed, chaotic night
will conquer it. In the course of the series we are told
that night wells up from the lower realms of the human
being, an ocean of blood. Mind disintegrates—all that
mankind has gained in long hours of thought dissolves.

Here again a strange mythological story unfolds. By

the powers of light and thought man has been divided
from his true home which is the realm of dreams and
darkness. Reaching out for the very throne of God
(*eritis sicut Deus* . . .) he boasts of his light. He laughs
at the ominous writing on the wall. But suddenly from
the very womb of night a black fog arises to engulf him
in untold suffering. The gods do not help; they reside in
splendor and turn away from pain. Now man feels the
bondage of guilt and suffering; this, however, is the
beginning of his salvation, for only he who has been up
to his neck in the swamp knows what longing for purity
means. But the poet sees resurrection merely as a dream,
not as conscious reality: consciousness and reality are
dead, and night has prevailed. She slays weakness and
strength alike; finally she removes injury and disgust
from the noble but does not give him any hope that
ultimate destruction can be avoided. He is struck dumb
with the great horror of annihilation.

Sometimes, indeed, he sees man clinging to a rock in
a dark ocean—but he is soon sucked back into the vortex
of destruction. He is forced to give up the heritage of
the day: individual thought and intellect. The ancient
forces of dream, intoxication, emotion, and blood will
govern again.

These somber and turbulent experiences are enhanced
by the austere imagery through which they are pre-
sented. Weinheber uses metaphor sparingly; only the
"day" and "night" images abound, and a muted atmos-
phere prevails in the chambers of his mind. He likes for
his similes the lute, the harp, and the flute. An aristo-
cratic touch is given by the symbols of sword, bow, and
arrow. Pitchers, a glass, goblets, bronze—these we
glimpse as we explore his imaginative household. In the
classic manner, he prefers generalized aspects of things.

For the landscape: clouds, stars, the moon, streams, trees, mountains, the abyss, rocks, the wind, flowers. Many of his images are taken from the life of the sea— boats, sails, islands, tides, waves. Occasionally he turns to mathematical concepts: the circle and the straight line. Strange is the nearly total absence of metaphors from the animal kingdom. The white deer is an exception. Seldom do we see a bird or hear rushing wings. Weinheber seems to have felt this curious lack: in *Zwischen Göttern und Dämonen* he says that the symbol of the bird has become meaningless, for that of beautiful youth has superseded it. A parallel suggests itself with the nineteenth-century Swiss poet C. F. Meyer—who lives in an imaginative world as cool and aristocratic as Weinheber's; he, also, is without hope and a fatalist.

As with Meyer, we find in Weinheber's writings practically no descriptions of living beings; the few portraits we have try to recreate distant or dead women: his mother, he says, has "the heavy dark hair of the Empress" (Elizabeth of Austria).

But though he rarely describes woman, he often mentions her. Sometimes she appears as the female who lures and traps man, and cheats him of his spiritual heritage; sometimes as a dream-created phantom of delight. He also sees her as the warm motherly house-wife. Though he does not describe individual women, he uses the device of translating their essence into an image, usually of a landscape or a flower. He did not, of course, invent this device, but it recurs so often in his poems as to become a mannerism. He seems to be conscious of this peculiarity of his imaginative faculty, and a section of *Adel und Untergang* is entitled "Human Landscapes." Here are some of the images into which real people translate themselves in his mind.

Description of a young girl: a gentle countryside, in the beginning of spring; innocent meadows; sometimes the wind stirs the flowers; time passes as in a dream, and forms and shadows wander there, hand in hand. This first part parallels closely a poem by Verlaine, "Clair de lune": *Votre âme est un paysage choisi—Que vont charmants masques et bergamasques. . . .* Unlike the French poet, who in the course of the poem seems to forget that he is describing a soul and becomes lost in the moonlit landscape, Weinheber deliberately stays by his task. We remain conscious of the "young girl" as he goes on with more details: a quiet lake, cool, and not deep; the skies are mirrored in it.

In a similar vein he describes a youth: an austere wind over brown hills. Flighty spring trembles and sobs in the grass. Clouds on slack bridles trail over a sky of blue glass. A heron lifts himself on slender wings into the morning air. About him the fiery young day breaks in flames.

Portrait of a woman: Daisies murmur on the hillside. A linden tree stands broad and fragrant. A smell of bread and warmth is in the air. Poppies glow like a ripe mouth. A lark, full of passion, sings high in the glassy air, while heavy sap pulses up from dark roots of trees and fills the stem.

Portrait of a man: a lonely island, rocks, and the sea. The stubborn sound of the surf. A storm from the dunes, the sky like steel. A boat at the shore, the oars in readiness, a sword in the boat. Sea gulls try their strong wings.

It is easily seen that these "translations" of human beings into landscapes do not refer to individual characters. Verlaine's poem, on the contrary, gives the poet's impression of one distinct person, and as he describes her (we assume it is a woman) he grows more and more at one with her and with the landscape; the reader becomes part of this fusion of personality and landscape, so that in the end a magic effect of transmutation is achieved. This is not true of Weinheber's "translations." We are continually conscious of what is going on—it is more like an interesting mental exercise than poetry. In fact one feels that given a little practice one might easily translate one's own impressions into such images —not, of course, so expertly phrased.

While the slightly pedantic "Human Landscapes" are not Weinheber at his best, he shows a more individual touch when he describes real landscape. Here we get some graphic descriptions, otherwise so conspicuously lacking in his work. He remembers the stale surroundings which filled his youth with hatred. A suburban view is typical:

> Die gelben Häuser stauen sich an dem Rand.
> Die Stadt mit müden Brauen erlischt im Land.
> Der Wiesen Haut zerfressen in Gärten klein
> schrumpft schwarz vom Gift der Essen wie Wundenbrand.
>
> .   .   .   .
>
> Der Abend schluckt Gesichter wie Pillen ein
> Am Hang die ersten Lichter sind krank und klein.
> Der Wind vom Friedhof raubt sich den bittren Duft
> der Toten und bestaubt sich mit morschem Bein.*

*The yellow houses totter at the brim.
 The city, weary-browed, grows wan and dim.
 The meadow's skin, devoured with garden plots,
 Shrinks black like poison wounds with gangrened rim.

.   .   .   .   .   .

 The evening eats all faces like doctor's pills,
 The first small lights glow sickly from the hills.
 Wind from the churchyard brings a stale perfume,
 Dust from decayed bones hangs in his quills.

Vereinsamtes Herz, p. 22.

His disgust for the surroundings of the hard years of his adolescence and young manhood persists. The tree at his window was brown and half eaten by caterpillars. His tiny room contained only a lumpy cot, a crooked chest swarming with moths, a bookshelf housing Virgil, Horace, *Faust*, Dickens, and the *Iliad*. His descriptions here are very detailed. Misery seems to have engraved these pictures indelibly on his mind, and they are more tangible than the happy landscape of his childhood, mentioned earlier: a faraway land, light clouds; on the pastures of heaven a beautiful moon and countless stars; broad, waving meadows; the soft silk of wind-swept grain. These seem rather nostalgic dreams than real horizons, skies, or meadows. In this enchanted land he still lives with his dead mother, but it has no refreshing or reviving power for him; he says himself that these memories cannot last in the wildness of life. They are, he feels, in the same sphere with the consolations of religion, also unattainable. But they will come to him, he hopes, in the hour of death. He is quite conscious of the fact that landscapes influence him strongly; the scenes of his adolescence, he says, were not landscapes— they served only as a half-noticed background to the wanton and bitter experiences of his youth. Later, Assisi becomes the setting of his manhood. Here, he says, hard and tender hands of men have shaped the face of the earth for centuries. Here is found innocent freedom. Eternal cypresses guard the past of destroyed temples. The clouds stand still, a flute sounds. An eagle soars high in golden space. A mature heart may dream here of its real home. Again, this would seem not the realistic description of a landscape but rather a symbol of poetic longing.

Often he describes flowers. But he does not make us

see their shape or their color. It is a reversal of his "Human Landscapes": the flowers call up images of human beings. The anemone is the soul in a pale girl's face, the tulip reminds him of a buxom country maid, loved by everyone in the village. Other flowers become symbols of human qualities: the miracle of the dandelion shows the noble endurance of misunderstood and unnoticed beauty. The thistle is the image of his own experience, to be sniffed and eventually eaten by any lame donkey, he says wryly.

Though in these short poems touches of humor appear, and a certain gusto for the warm, pleasant things of life comes out, as in the cited description of a woman, the main impression from Weinheber's poetic output must be that of somber turbulence, of dark and tempestuous emotions.

It is evident that this poet envisages a victory of dark forces, which to him are very real. The tide of blood from the realms of the subconscious is destined to engulf the thin light of intellect—chaos will smother the individual, who submits in fascination and terror.

The main source of this attitude is no doubt the deeply disturbed European scene. But personal influences enter in. Weinheber's life has been hampered not merely by the adverse circumstances of birth and a lonely youth but also by his unprepossessing appearance: pictures show him as an uncouth man of nondescript features. From the beginning the poet must have felt that everything was against him and that the only calm and lovely thing in life would always be his art. Conscious of his unusual gifts, he is very bitter on the subject of his early lack of recognition and often seeks consolation in drink. His feeling of frustration appears even in the title of one of his collections: *Späte Krone*—"Belated Crown." Carossa calls his own volume simply *Collected Poems*. But Weinheber's more flamboyant titles are well in keeping with his general style.

Another title, *Adel und Untergang*—"Nobility and Destruction"—embodies the main issues of his philosophy: on one side the virtues of courage and nobility, which must be upheld at any price, without thought of reward; on the other, dark and victorious annihilation. This bright nobility of man is balanced precariously between the gods and the demons.

The poet's deepest dedication is to the power and sacredness of language, though the identification of language and Folk may well be called fantastic, and we have little evidence that he carries out his own precepts of conscious creation. It is tragic that a man so haunted by the dark forces of the unconscious should strive so hard, and withal so unsuccessfully, for clear consciousness.

The world he sees around him also has an aspect of unresolved duality: his realistic descriptions of hated scenes contrast sharply with the dreamlike quality of the landscapes he loves. We miss in his work the charming intimacy with plant and animal life so often found in German poetry and so evident in Carossa. Never thoroughly at home in the reality of his surroundings, Weinheber fails to establish any abiding certainty, or even the hope of it; the subconscious urge toward disintegration proves stronger than his sporadic attempts to fulfill a mission of preservation conceived by his intellect.

While Carossa seeks to preserve values through the medium of his art, Weinheber feels that art and language in themselves are the values to be preserved. And in his own way he does keep alive the heritage of the past; for his is a long and distinguished ancestry: classic meters, French symbolism, the austere splendors of Stefan George and of the earlier C. F. Meyer, the choice imagery of Rilke—these and others we recognize. And as regards content, the wrenching fear that reality as we know it is meaningless and will be destroyed harks back to the Expressionists. Nor has Weinheber, in his turn, been able to build a new world.

A man caught within the confines of his own soul, he pays little heed to the happenings around him. Unable to identify himself with a group, he sees himself as the proud and lonely one, and in his seclusion probably knows little of the more sinister elements in his immediate surroundings. The story is told of how he was once found, by a reporter seeking an interview, tossing incoherently on a couch in the corner of a room. He had given no answer to a knock at the door and responded as little to a question. *"Geh'n Se weg,"* muttered the poet, *"ich dichte."* ("Go away, I'm making poetry.") The anecdote suggests well enough the absorbed and passionate life of this strange, bitter, ugly man.

His background, and the natural caution of one whose entire history has been a struggle for existence, may well explain why there are so few references in his poems to present events. We have seen that his extolling of "beautiful youth" is marked by a reversal of meaning in the "night" symbolism, indicating that we have here an artificial construction. The reference to a "terrible Lord of the Earth" may or may not apply to persons now living. However, the general atmosphere of impending doom and of hopelessness is certainly the product of his European setting.

In the end it is perhaps only fair to measure Weinheber by his own standards: the highest value he knows is beauty of language. And in its preservation he ranks with the best. He is deeply devoted to his art, and the perfection of his style will do much to carry classic beauty through a time so dangerous to every form of creativeness.

ALBERT STEFFEN

OUR third poet, Albert Steffen, was born in Switzer-
land in 1884; like Carossa, the son of a physician.
He spent the happy days of his childhood on the
banks of the Aare, a lively river which runs through the
Swiss Jura, eventually joining the Rhine. This landscape,
while without the austere majesty of the high Alps, has a
charm peculiarly its own: the river winds through a
fertile valley bordered by hills crowned with old castles,
while in the background rise the wooded ranges of the
Jura Mountains, dark and threatening by day, softly
violet when night approaches.

With his young friends Albert lived the life of a
country boy, running barefoot over the meadows, swim-
ming in the swift river. As a student he devoted himself
to natural science, beginning his study in the beautiful
cities of Berne and Lausanne. Then an urge not to be
denied drove him to Berlin, where he deliberately chose
to live in the most dismal quarter he could find, in the
north of the great city, among working people. He says:
"In order to understand life in all its depth, I took rooms
in a street where misery and sordidness prevailed. My
room looked out on a back yard on which the doors of an
inn opened. At night, I heard a bawling and screeching
that never ceased." Though he did not set foot in the
inn, the misery of its frequenters became a vivid ex-
perience for him. "I heard in this cry from within the
submergence of the human soul. It was like a call for
help, a clinging, a pressing demand to find the word of
salvation."[47]

During these years Steffen made a special study of
occupational diseases and pondered deeply the meaning

of sickness in human life. At this time his development
as a novelist began, the first step in a writing career
which has continued until the present day. He abandoned
the technical study of science, although retaining a
strong, self-informing interest in it. Unlike Carossa,
Steffen had no need of another profession and was able
to devote his full time to writing and other activities of
his choice. In 1923 he became editor of *Das Goetheanum*,
organ of the Anthroposophical Society. This periodical
became well known in Europe for its general cultural
breadth and its searching articles on topics of philosophy,
art, literature, and religion. Like the Society itself, it has
been forbidden in Germany, but still has a large circula-
tion in England. Steffen's connection with this publica-
tion and the Society drew him to Dornach in Switzerland,
where he lives today.

Steffen occupies a unique place in the world of German
literature: he is a representative of modern mysticism
and easily the most significant Swiss poet of the day.
His works, moreover, have not been put on the index in
Germany, although they cannot by any stretch of the
imagination be taken as supporting the present regime.
The list of his publications—dramas, essays, novels, and
poems—is the impressive token of a fertile, creative life.
We are here concerned only with his lyric poetry.

The deepest impulse of this poet has always been
toward a modern form of mysticism, or perhaps one
should say, rather, a form of mysticism possible to a man
living fully the life of our time. In his development along
this line he has identified himself more and more with
the teachings of Rudolf Steiner, 1861–1925. As he him-
self says, not the direction but the pace and intensity of
his spiritual evolution have been profoundly influenced
by this inspired teacher. We must pause for a moment to

consider the meaning of this "modern mysticism" and the nature of Dr. Steiner's contribution.

This Austrian scholar and mystic early became dissatisfied with the theosophical movement with which he had been associated and turned into a path of his own, in an effort to enable modern man to free himself from half-understood doctrines in the field of esoteric study, approaching it in the spirit of impartial research—not accepting anything on authority, but expecting everything from conscious individual experience. This ultimately brought to mystical tradition in Europe an entirely new impetus, and Dr. Steiner has come to be recognized by esoterics as one of the great masters of metaphysical thought. In stressing the words "individual" and "conscious," we emphasize two of the main concepts that characterize Dr. Steiner's teachings, which have come to bear the impressive title of Anthroposophy. (Steiner himself, abhorring set terms, would have liked to give a different name to his philosophy every week, so that no one could become a "disciple.") It will be noted that the condition expressed in the word "conscious" distinguishes Anthroposophy from any form of mediumistic occultism. The term "individual," on the other hand, sets this approach to insight apart from Buddhism, with which it otherwise has much in common. In Dr. Steiner's conception of the world, the possibility of self-realization for the individual derives in its deepest implications from the sacrifice of Christ: that is, the mystical and complete gift of life which lies in the willingness of Deity to go through the bitter experience of mortal life and death for the sake of mankind.

For Dr. Steiner individual consciousness is the highest gift of the divine powers to humanity, and although in his version of the mystic's discipline extrasensual experience is sought, the process of active thinking may never be relinquished. On the contrary—it is through meticulous observation of the most exacting rules for clear thinking that ultimately the individual may gain strength to come into contact with divine power, and to understand the creative process of the universe.

Parallel to this education in active thinking must go a strict self-education in the spheres of emotion and of will. Self-possession, or as near an approach to it as is possible to the individual, is the goal of an effort which must be maintained according to tested rules and over a period of years. One of the effects of this process is the separation, and more and more distinct experience, of the faculties of thought, feeling, and will (which in ordinary experience are commonly confused and blurred, with resulting confusion in the individual's inner life). This means that the seeker after truth will come to a point where he can have experience without the interference of roused emotions, and where no impulse toward action will flow into him from any outside source. He will then be completely "detached."

The methods that have been found efficient in bringing about the desired development are set forth fully, even pedantically, in Dr. Steiner's writings.[48] A danger arising in the course of this discipline is, obviously, that one may become cold and develop a deadly form of higher egotism; in the language of some occult societies, this would be the beginning of the "black path." Such a contingency must be forestalled by conscious direction of emotional life, and an exacting moral self-training. If all that pertains to this phase of spiritual development is strictly observed, man will find at the point where outside influences stop a rush of power from his innermost being, whose source is the universal living Christ.

As this state is attained, all action will be prompted by principle for its own sake, unaffected by self-consideration or any other motives such as fear or hatred. The individual will then be truly "free."

We have called this conception of life "mysticism." But both Steffen and Steiner lack the emotional exaltation usually connected with the mystic approach to religious experience. The impression created is rather that of an alpine landscape, austere, clear, and cool, but made friendly by the brilliance of the sun and by flowers unknown to lower regions.

The emphasis on consciousness in this philosophy is carried over into what Albert Steffen considers the mission of a poet. He sees our position in modern life as a peculiar and difficult one. We are becoming sensitive to the fact that the world which actually makes our environment is more and more meaningless to us. Under the hands of our poets the visible and tangible reality dissolves. Before our uneasy eyes old values have grown empty; new ones of similar depth and sureness of meaning have not replaced them.

As recently as in the times of our great-grandfathers people still had a deep and satisfying relation with the things around them. They would feel, for instance, the living reality of the well on their farm. The water coming up from the depth of the earth, brought to light by the exertion of their own strength—the memories of their ancestors who dug this well—dry summers, and times of flood—all this lived in their subconscious feeling when they heard the word "well." For us, living now in civilized surroundings, the word merely spells a primitive and uncomfortable form of existence. To the country woman also it means a yearning to move to the city and profit by an easier form of life. But what do we experience when we hear the corresponding word "faucet"? Probably irritation: There the thing goes dripping again—have to get a new washer—as though we didn't pay enough for city water as it is . . . etc., etc.

This is the state in which civilized man finds himself: things formerly full of meaning seem dead, or simply irritating; our relation with "nature" is broken, and we say that we live in a machine age. Poetry dealing with nature, or those "things" which have been immemorially bound up with the closeness of nature to our lives, has to a great extent lost its appeal because no experience in our own soul meets it. There is no doubt that poetry can be written about machines, and it has been written very well indeed. But (and here is the crux of the matter) the poet cannot rely on a wealth of experience that fills our subconscious and semiconscious mind, to be awakened by certain words; he is obliged to create very consciously, and to throw a kind of grappling hook into the sphere of the intellect, on which the understanding of his poetry will then depend. All of which is very dangerous to poetry. This is why "machine poets" often stress the social effect of the machine rather than its realistic function: here at least they are assured of an emotional response, although their poetry is then apt to be labeled propaganda, and the author imagined as a radical. Other modern poets use the actual rhythm of the machine, getting a nervous response similar to the effect of jazz. They bludgeon us into a semiconscious state, quite agreeable to many people but detrimental to clear thinking. All these capable poets address themselves only to parts of the human being and use only parts of the life around us. But the poet who still wants to convey something of the wholeness of human life to the whole human being is confronted with a difficult task. "Things" do not help him any more—if they are to have life, he has to create it.

This seems to be the import of some rather mysterious lines we find already in the Ninth Elegy of Rilke:

> Mehr als je
> fallen die Dinge dahin, die erlebbaren, denn
> was sie verdrängend ersetzt, ist ein Tun ohne Bild.*

The earth wants to become "invisible"—the poet must transform "the things" in his own heart into himself—whoever he may be in the end. Then come the significant lines:

> Erde, ist es nicht dies, was du willst: unsichtbar
> in uns erstehn? . . .
> Was, wenn Verwandlung nicht, ist dein drängender Auftrag?†

And in the Seventh Elegy we hear, even more clearly, the death knell of the visible world:

> Nirgends, Geliebte, wird Welt sein, als innen.
> . . . Und immer geringer
> schwindet das Aussen.‡

The experience is by no means new. Goethe felt the approach of this poetical dearth even in his time, when "things" still had meaning to most human beings. In *Faust I* we have a scene where he curses everything in life and declares it worthless. Then a chorus of spirits

---

*More than ever the things that might be experienced diminish, for what, crowding them out, takes their place is action sans image. R. M. Rilke, *Duineser Elegien*, *Ausgewählte Werke* (Leipzig, 1938), Vol. I.

†Earth, is it not this you want: to be resurrected in us, invisible? . . . What is your urgent mission if not transformation?

‡Nowhere, beloved, will there be world except in us. . . . And ever diminished the outer world dwindles.

sing that Faust, having destroyed the beautiful world, must now build it up, more powerful and more splendid, in his own breast.

Steffen has given much thought to this plight of poetry. It is in vain, he feels, to wait for "inspiration" as Rilke did through troubled years, although he recognizes the gift of poetry as a grace of God. However, this grace will not come any longer if the human being does not prepare for it, just as a plowman prepares the field, knowing that growth will indeed come by the forces of nature but only if he does his part. The poet, Steffen tells us, must acquire consciously the approach to nature that was freely accessible to a more naïve age.

In the critical essay, "Der Weg des Dichters,"[49] he gives an account of a possible way to come to a poetic realization of nature. We may examine with interest this discipline of the perceptions intended to stretch and deepen the awareness from which an integrated poetic faculty springs.

The poet will free his ego from every outside influence; he will seek his master not in other human beings, or trends of thought, or ancient or modern rules of art, but only in his own inner heart. Nature herself is to be his guide. From the point of view of science nature is in a sense inert, a meaningless dance of "forces"; from the point of view of religion nature is sinful, in that it is gross, unspiritualized matter. The poet must find his own approach. He will offer to her three things: a plant, a mineral, and an animal, and see what nature herself says through them.

At first the poet contemplates a tiny seed and follows its natural development in his own thoughts: It is given to the earth; small roots shoot down, the germ shoots upward. Leaves develop, a stem grows high—the delicate flower unfolds, which by and by changes into the hard seed pods. The Word of nature goes through seed, germ, leaf, chalice, and fruit, as an eternal principle.

Here the source in Goethe's "Metamorphose der Pflanzen" is evident, and Steffen would not deny this. He sees in Goethe's philosophy a trend akin to his own and admits that he is himself in search of the *Urpflanze* which Goethe "saw" with the eyes of his mind. When Goethe, the naïve realist, told Schiller, the idealist, of his Urpflanze, Schiller said characteristically: "This is not an experience, it is an idea." Goethe answered with some asperity: "Then I am glad that I can see an idea."

"Seeing an idea" is the aim of Steffen's experiment; it is not, of course, intended as a series of images poetically valuable—their use is that of a stimulus to awareness. Nor is it meant as the only conceivable train of images which might accomplish a deepened realization. One may note also that images which seem unconnected, sentimental, or fortuitous on the surface may make an instant bridge in the inner awareness of the thinker and so carry him along in much truer, swifter perception than he could derive from more verbally smooth and expressive passages.

To continue with the plant: The pale network of tiny roots reminds us not of the sun but of the moon. The spiral growth of leaves is like the staff of Mercury, the messenger, who leads us up to Venus, rising in the flower. So the forces which move the planets come into our mind, and above them all we feel vividly the power of the sun whose light directs the heavenly orchestra.

It calls forth the vast chorus of small guardian spirits which enliven nature and reveal themselves to a poet. In the depth, among rocks, sand, and loam, the poet's imagination discovers little gnomes with enormous heads. They are superintelligent—without needing logical proof they perceive at once the most intricate systems of thought. They suggest epigrams, aphorisms, these little creatures who are close to the immense, compact fertilities of the earth; they inspire satirists.

As we again fix our attention on the leaves and on the stem of the flower, we lose sight of the gnomes and a soft, flowing mood takes hold of us. As the life stream of the plant surges up, we feel as though waves were carrying us along, rocking us into a state of semi-consciousness. Through this aspect of the plant we perceive ourselves in the realm of Undine, the kingdom of the waters. Here, we feel, is the home of odes.

But on the colorful blossoms nymphs are singing their songs—no consonants bring harshness, only soft, ineffable vowels float around us. They sing love songs.

The flower matures into the seed, and the ancient salamander, the silent one, keeps a secret for the quietest souls: Christ himself has given us the metaphor in a grain of wheat—his body is our bread.

If the poet, so Steffen tells us, will submit to the discipline of this "exercise" he will feel his mental nimbleness increase. And indeed, we should not criticize his prescription before we have tried it.

Steffen further tells us that the poet who takes these teachings to heart will have a more diversified reaction toward his fellow beings; he will know them more intimately; his emotional and imaginative reaction will be intensified and flexible. Reading a book on modern psychoanalysis, for instance, he may suddenly see before his mind's eye a swamp with stagnant pools, blue dragonflies, green frogs, and he will feel himself sinking. In reading abstract political programs, he may see a blind alley of houses not yet finished but already in ruins. In other words, with thought about all varieties of things he will begin to have a spontaneous accompaniment of imagination and feeling. But this is not poetry. The author is here in danger of becoming addicted to allegories, built up out of casual association. He is losing the firm ground under his feet and must counteract this tendency. For poetry means insight, depth of awareness, not merely loose association.

The poet will return to the study of nature. This time the mineral shall be his guide, but he is not going to put his mind to analysis of the material—this would kill his poetic perception of a more vital sort. He will begin by imagining that nature asks him to shape her image in different metals, and will follow the dictates of his material in creating the image. Matter, as nature herself tells him, is the equivalent of *mater*—it is the motherly foundation of all life.

Iron will be his first material. The head he shapes is angular, bony. The lips are hard. The expression of this head is cold, clear, intellectual—fear pervades him who beholds it. Deep insight into the nature of iron will be granted to the artist who contemplates this image.

He chooses copper next. The face that emerges is gentle, compassionate. Raphael, the archangel who inspires the physician, leads us to help the unfortunate and the sick. If silver is chosen as material, nature will assume the features of the madonna. The stress in all these experimental images lies on the material: the artist must not conceive first an abstract image—he must allow the material to be his guide. Then his works will have reality.

The poet, after studying the possibilities of material in this way, will then return to human life, and subject

it to a close scrutiny—he will learn with insatiable
curiosity the industrial origin of objects surrounding
him. He will know how chairs are manufactured, how
paper, food—everything around him—is made. He will
also familiarize himself with all professions, which are
the material of life, and be at home in the workroom of a
seamstress as well as in the barbershop or the factory.
Only then can he lay claim to master epic art.

Some of these precepts, of course, are not new—any
course teaching short-story writing will advise young
authors to become familiar with their surroundings.
But the method here is more than usually concentrated
and more continually conscious. Just as, in our childhood,
we learn laboriously to write, and later write effortlessly
without ever remembering the first shaping of our
letters, so the poet is learning the medium of his
creativeness. The ordinary man, in regard to vivid sense
of the reality of things, is largely in the process of
shaping—with huge effort—the separate letters of ex-
perience. This is why the ordinary imagination tires so
quickly in any prolonged effort of focus.

So far, the poet has learned from the plant something
of the depth and spirit which underlie the writing of
lyrics; in thinking of the minerals he will have stretched
himself to certain kinds and breadths of insight necessary
to epic art. From the animal kingdom the elements of
drama emerge. For the form of an animal is the exact
mirror of its inner nature; we see its character in its
physiognomy. If we turn to the expressiveness of birds,
we see by analogy what in human beings reminds us of
the peacock, what of the sparrow. The lion shows a
high-headed readiness of passion; there is murder in the
stealth of the tiger. Cattle, heavy and somnolent, are
made for patient sacrificial death—they cannot escape

like the eagle or fight like the lion. In all these the poet will learn to contemplate parts of human nature—aspects of character or experience—and will come to discern more clearly the interplay of inner traits and qualities in the tangle of human life.

The final step the poet must take is his own self-education as a responsible moral and loving being. This is not a new idea; Schiller among others has postulated, as did also Goethe and Tolstoi, the ethical human being as the only true artist. What Steffen envisages is a constant and conscious effort of self-training; however, this is remote from ascetic practices, which withdraw the vital energy from genius.

Above all, the poet must be completely individual and true to his own experiences. Even when he would like to discard or embellish certain things he has done in his life, he must remain in a sense faithful to them and keep all his memories alive, consciously reliving them from time to time. By this process there filters through to the inner being a real awareness of where experience has been wrong, where true and right, and in what degree, and why. Only the continual inner chemistry of aware-ness makes possible an approach to truth; when we hide from our experience, or put it behind us through embar-rassment or disagreement or pain, we come away with an inert fragment in our hands and do not grow. To flee from our past is to weaken ourselves. Only if we remain mercilessly conscious of everything we have done and honest in admitting every cranny of our motives shall we find the way to improve ourselves and atone for our misdeeds. Only if the poet is true to his past, facing all of it with an open heart, can he become a master of the future; through his expanded understanding of the inner nature and relation of things, a vision of what is meant by the day of judgment will rise before his eyes and only then will he see the significance of the future. As he himself learns to judge and direct his own life, so he will understand the power of Christ, and as he endeavors to conquer evil by good so he will see the final victory of the forces of light. He will then have become a prophet, which is the true function of the poet.

It is likely that many authors would shudder at the thought of using what appear to be mental exercises in order to summon the muse. We saw that Carossa felt this shrinking, and indeed Steffen himself relates Rilke's reactions to his own ideas. During the years of the first World War Steffen was in Munich.[50] He often ate in a certain little restaurant and sometimes noticed there a slender, distinguished-looking man who quickly ate his simple meal and went his way without seeming to pay attention to anyone, though there were very interesting people among the habitués. His personality appeared metaphorically to Steffen thus:

His forehead seemed like a tower. The watchman sees from it a phantom army of Islamic angels. His mouth was strange like the mouth of a brook barb which Steffen often had watched with pleasure in his childhood. The fish used to stand in the clear water while little waves ran over the glistening pebbles. Suddenly Steffen understood the changing light in Rilke's eyes—they were clear sometimes, and sometimes shadowy like the water of the brook. They showed the change from trust to fear. Here, Steffen thought, is a spirit which, though free, feels that terror lies in wait for him—the fear of being torn from the very element of his life.

This description shows us what Steffen means when he speaks of translating impressions into images. He soon learned that the stranger was Rilke. One day Rilke took a seat at Steffen's table and engaged him in conversation. They talked about the war; Rilke told a touching story of his friend the Expressionist Kokoschka, a dragoon in the army: when riding to an attack he covered his horse's eyes with his hand so that the beast would be protected from the horror around them. In the course of the conversation Steffen said he thought that conscious knowledge would make a poet more productive—but immediately felt Rilke drawing back from the idea. When the younger man thought about the conversation later on, he came to the conclusion that a kind of uncertainty, which in spite of all his admiration he felt in Rilke's poems, resulted from this attitude.

There is no doubt that Rilke was no prophet in the sense we have outlined—he is rather like an aeolian harp, infinitely sensitive, infinitely vulnerable and at the mercy of "things." And yet Rilke himself, and Rodin, as we have seen in the study of Carossa, had a technique for deepening their awareness of the essential nature of things so closely parallel to Steffen's as to seem almost identical in purpose. In fact, Carossa couples Rilke's approach with Anthroposophy in discussing the matter, and in that case it is Carossa who turns away from both, feeling that they are essentially the same thing.

Whatever one's opinion of the mission of a poet, it is revealing to see how such a modern as Steffen trains his faculties. How the method works can only be ascertained by the individual, giving it fair trial and seeing the result. Perhaps it is safe to say that the path to deepened awareness is apt to differ in its outward details for those who trace it out for themselves and follow it; it must often be hard in superficial contact to cross the barriers of minor differences—repellent in themselves—to common awareness of the process involved. In this case we do not know whether the lack of agreement between Steffen and Rilke was the result of a superficial hazard of conversation—as for instance, the use of such a word as "knowledge" in varying sense—or more fundamental. But an analysis of Steffen's poems will give us some indication of what with him has been the result of this approach: what realities he describes, and how the world appears through the medium of his consciousness.

As might be expected in a poet who feels that "things" will indeed die if we do not give them meaning, there are very few external descriptions of objects or persons in Albert Steffen's poems. The realities he sees are realities of the spirit, though the steppingstone to these experiences is his own perception.

The only time he gives a clear description of a woman, he does so in conscious imitation of Impressionist technique: A black dress, a veiled hat, lace at her throat—so a woman appears to your mind's eye. A lovely everyday picture has been created by you, Steffen tells the Impressionist. But, he goes on, her angel must pass you by because you have only seen her as a woman. From a purple flood a deeply frightened, starry face looks out; but you have missed the vision of her fate.[51]

In many instances, description immediately turns into inner vision. He sees for instance a landscape in the fog; the moon is a shallow pond, the sky is hidden, and the pale pond no longer reflects the purpose of the gods. Ever denser becomes the fog that hides the heavens—but we must find the divine light of love in our own heart. Then the sufferings of nature will cease, for the state of nature mirrors the spiritual condition of man. This poem[52] is typical of many of Steffen's lyrics: deep discouragement brought about by the attempt to find inspiration in the world around us, a decided effort of the will, and the solution—strength must be found in our own heart. This shows typically the sequence: emptiness of the world—until we find its life in our heart only.

Viewed from another angle we see the inverse of the process, where another solution must be found. In the poem "Die Waldbewohner" ("Denizens of the Forest")[53] the poet has a vision of the spirits imprisoned in nature. There they lie in the dark woods, held by roots in granite rocks—a smell of blood and dissolution is in the air. A wheel with spokes of fire turns in the depth. The dream shows him souls frozen into the rock—and his own soul is scorched by fire—ghosts approach in flames, and his bones freeze at the sight. All these creatures, so the poet feels, are imprisoned in the deep recesses of his soul, and they accuse him because he has not delivered them by bringing them light. He can save them only by opening his eyes and going out into the world.

There is no real contradiction between these opposed views; the two poems typify the two ways open to the mystic: the way into the macrocosm, the known world of nature and the stars where the reality of Man will appear, and the way into the microcosm, into our own heart, where the nature of things will be revealed. His dream-vision has enabled him to see beyond the sensual appearance and to perceive the inner meaning. Reality is strengthened and made more vivid by the vision, which in turn would have been impossible without loving contemplation of the creatures of the earth.

Time and again Albert Steffen stresses one thing: life on earth, with all its suffering and all its joy must be lived consciously. Viewed in the light of divine purpose,

even the simplest task becomes important. He shows
this in one of his poems:[54] A human soul comes to rest
at the grave of Christ. But the poet tells her that resur-
rection, not death, must be her goal. She must not weep
at the cross; she must take its wood and build with it a
house. Christ was a carpenter, and if the human soul is
willing to become an apprentice, a journeyman, and
finally a master carpenter, all good spirits will help.
Christ is always very near to man, and indeed he is the
activating force in even his humblest undertaking.

In a poem of uncommon charm Steffen expresses the
meaning of suffering:

> Du denkst, dein Leiden hätte keinen Wert.
> —Doch in der Nacht, da naht ein Geisterzug
> und schaut in dich und sieht ein weisses Pferd
> auf schwarzem Ackerland, vor goldnem Pflug,
> hochaufgebäumt, und seine Zügel hält
> ein Kind, das Antlitz überströmt von Blut.
> "—Du leidest für die unterirdische Welt,
> für jeden Toten, der im Grabe ruht."*

Here, without stimulus from any sensuous experience,
a consoling perception is given a poignantly accurate
image.

In many poems the relation of human beings to the
earth is shown in the form of a vision. Once we see the

*You think your suffering is valueless;
  But in the night there comes a spirit train,
  Looks into you and sees there a white horse
  On a black field, drawing a golden plow.
  The horse rears high, and lo, its reins are held
  By a young child, his face suffused with blood.
  "You suffer for the subterranean world,
  And for each dead that rests within the grave."
                    Wegzehrung (Basel, 1922), p. 98.

poet abandoning his home and crossing the river of death. He journeys in the company of a gnome. But their boat is magically attracted to a mountain of many-colored jewels, and the poet becomes a child on the journey. At the magic mountain a giant woman gives him all her jewels. But he decides not to stay—"true to the earth I bend my mind on my return."[55]

The conscious turning to the earth has a prototype in Faust's decision to return to life on earth after contemplating suicide—and a curious contrast in Werther's decision to leave the earth as "he is given to the father, not to the son."

The fate of earth, dimly felt by Weinheber and sensed by the delicate perception of Rilke, is explored by Steffen in several poems. He uses the term *Entwerdende Erde*[56]—an expression difficult to translate. *Werden* is "to become," and the prefix *ent* usually means "out of" or "away from." It would mean here that the earth has lost the possibility of development, that its life is stagnant, or even retrogressive. But at the same time Steffen says characteristically that man, carrying out the plans of the gods, can change the destiny of earth.

Similar ideas are given in several other poems, of which we will analyze one more. Here man tries to find the forces that will help him to save himself, but the earth does not yield them—the lily with the white blossom does not rise from the dark earth. He sets sail in the silver light of the moon to wash his soul in the light of the past—he finds only dust and ashes. His spirit is stifled in dark craters. But in the heights of heaven Christ speaks to the Father and is sent down to build in the dark tomb windows, which look out upon the palace of the sun, with a free view in all directions, so that man may see the light with his own eyes.[57]

The position of man on earth is not as Weinheber sees it, "between the gods and the demons." Steffen's conception is more subtle. Man stands between two demons; if he can find and keep the balanced way between them, he will identify himself with Christ:

> Es schlingen deine Tat ins Labyrinth
> Zwei Wesen, eines Feuer, eines Knochen.
> Du folgst, bald froh, bald bang, dein Herzepochen
> bringt dich zur Weltenmutter mit dem Kind.
> "Ist meine Tat ein gutes Angebind?
> Hab ich was Schreckliches damit verbrochen?
> Wird sie belohnt," denkst du, "wird sie gerochen?"
> Und weisst nicht, wer die Fragesteller sind.
> Es spricht das Kind: "Wer weckt die Eitelkeiten,
> dass du die Tat betrachtend, dich geniessest?
> O sieh, zu deiner Linken steht der Teufel.
> Und wer erzeugte Angst und Reu und Zweifel,
> dass du dich in die Selbstvernichtung stiessest?
> O sieh den Satan dir zur rechten Seiten."*

The Persian religion recognizes one of these demons as Ahriman—the other will be known to Christian esoterics as Lucifer. Here is an unusual conception of

*Two beings, one of fire and one of bone,
  Engulf your every action in a maze.
  You follow, now elated, now depressed,
  Your heartbeat finds the Mother with the Child.
  "My action—has it been a welcome gift?
  Or was a crime committed when I did it?
  Shall I be punished? Or shall I be praised?"
  You do not know who in you asks these questions.
  The Child says: "Who has wakened vanity,
  That savouring yourself you scan your actions?
  Oh see, at your left side the devil stands!
  Who roused you to such anguished doubt and terror,
  That you were driven to annihilation?
  Oh look! Satan himself stands at your right."

Wegzehrung, p. 61.

good and evil, based on Rudolf Steiner's philosophy. There is no dualism; we do not hover between gods and demons. Evil results if man is unable to strike the balance between forces which on the one side tempt him to vanity and extreme egotism—Lucifer, and on the other side would drive him to despair and self-annihilation— Ahriman. The scale of either, too heavily weighed down, will draw the human being to destruction. The beam that strikes a just balance is held by Christ. The new thought here, and one that is basic in the philosophy of both Steffen and Steiner, is that man cannot save himself by shunning some "evil" but must accept all of life and balance its forces within himself. Only in this way, Steffen feels, can man save the earth and carry out the plan of the progressive forces in the universe. For earth itself is in danger, as well as mankind. The responsibility rests squarely with man himself. No God will descend to save, unless we do our part. The powers of evil feed and grow strong on our evil thoughts, and the powers of good are nourished by our noble aspirations.

The typical course of occult experience is also given in a poem by Steffen.[58] The day has come—so the poet begins, making us realize that a long period of preparation has preceded the expected day. "The day has come when demons and angels flee from emptiness. They find nothing to build up or to tear down; they are afraid to be annihilated in me." The human being is completely alone. Up to now he has been guided by angels and preyed upon by demons. He has strengthened his individuality to such an extent that these outside influences can have no more hold on him. "Everywhere on earth I see being, but in myself being disappears and becomes non-being. Flight of the gods, cessation of fate, loss of will-power, indifference to all happening." This is

"complete emptiness," the goal also of Buddhist train-
ing. "This is the test of the spirit." Here within this
emptiness indeed the human being has to find and decide
what the real will of his own being is.

Goethe expresses the same experience in his alle-
gorical poem, "Zueignung." There he tells of a vision he
has had in the early morning hours, as he is ascending a
mountain. Out of the mist a wonderful form appears to
him—the vision of a great and beautiful woman. He
tells her that he has found truth for himself and will now
keep it sacred, not profaning it by showing it to the
multitude. But she only smiles. Suddenly he realizes his
selfishness and promises to give his truth to his fellow
men. He then receives the veil of poetry from the hands
of truth.

Fundamentally, although told in a "veiled" form, the
experience is the same as that related in Steffen's more
uncompromising poem. At the point where Steffen says,
"this is the test of the spirit," he also has a vision—not
of a beautiful woman, but of Christ, who tells him that
only he can give life.

While Goethe uses the veil of poetry, Steffen describes
the experiences which form the subjects of his poems
with relentless realism; we have to make a strenuous and
conscious effort to understand them, taking into con-
sideration the whole complex of Steffen's world. The
ideas themselves, however, the poet presents simply.
The world of his metaphors is not varied. The cross, the
stars, the rose and other flowers, trees, birds, especially
the eagle, the sun and moon; the lion and the steer, the
angel—these make up in large part the world of his
imagination. In his novels metaphors taken from science,
especially from medicine, are frequent; if a reader did

not know the author had studied natural sciences he would guess it from his vocabulary. But in his lyrics this realm is not touched.

His imagination is full of color; red, blue, silver, green, violet, gold, black, and white abound, with red appearing most frequently and blue a close second. These colors have an ancient meaning, and in some poems the symbolism is uncovered:

> Als wir auf der goldnen Insel schliefen,
> geistvereinter, ungeteilter Schau,
> lockte mich das Rot und dich das Blau,
> die zum Wollen und zum Wissen riefen.
>
> Aber da wir auseinander liefen,
> überwallte uns Gespenstergrau,
> und die Liebe zwischen Mann und Frau
> wurde Mord und Selbstmord in den Tiefen.
>
> Hart am Abgrund in der herbsten Not
> wölbte sich ein heilig weisser Bogen
> über das in Nacht gesunkne Eiland.
> Nicht vom Blau war er und nicht vom Rot,
> Nicht vom Gold der Insel hergezogen,
> Nur vom Auferstehungslicht im Heiland.*

*As we on the golden isle were sleeping,
 One in spirit, seeing all as one,
 Red called me and you were called by blue—
 Red called to the will, and blue to knowledge.

But as we ran far from each other
 We were swallowed up in spectral grey,
 And the love between a man and woman
 Turned to murder and to suicide.

Near the precipice, as we seemed lost,
 Stretched a bow of holy gleaming whiteness
 Over the island which had sunk in night.
 Not of blue it was, nor yet of red,
 Nor was it drawn from the island's gold.
 Light came from the resurrected Saviour.

Wegzehrung, p. 58.

The symbol of the white light is important. We find it often in romantic poetry. Shelley's "Adonais" contains these lines:

> The One remains, the many change and pass.
> Heaven's light for ever shines, Earth's shadows fly;
> Life, like a dome of many-colored glass
> Stains the white radiance of Eternity.

He identifies the unbroken white light with "eternity"; for Steffen, it signifies Christ. One is reminded here of the Neoplatonic scale of values: White light—*Nous*, or Spirit; colored light—*Logos*, Life; Darkness—*Hyle* or matter, a negative value.[59] Goethe's works also offer many references to a similar symbolism of colors. Indeed, his *Farbenlehre*, the result of eighteen years of study, opposes the mechanical theory of Newton in favor of more ancient doctrines about the nature of light. The same attitude is taken by many romantic poets, Blake, Shelley, Keats, and especially Coleridge.[60] In Steffen's poems we have a definite symbolic value for colors: blue, as the color of contemplation, of devotion, leads to knowledge; red, as the color of enthusiasm, of love, and of the will, leads to action. The predominance of red, the active color, would show that the conscious will of the individual has permeated his subconscious mind and colored the world of his imaginings.

Certain of Steffen's poems dealing with the symbols of the rose, cross, and other images belong to a rather special group. They cannot be analyzed as lyrics, and are not written simply to be read and enjoyed, but are again recipes for experience. They are meant for the purpose of meditation: that is, the voluntary inducement of a state of consciousness which enables man to have spiritual realization.* As might be expected of a poet who may be defined as a modern mystic, this group is large. The pattern is always the same: darkness, despair, the feeling that all is lost—then an effort of the will, and help from the divine powers which are waiting for just this human effort. We will outline only two of them.[61]

The first: A rose floats into the black melancholy of a sleepless night—a heart flames in the rose, and expands in four parts which unite to form a cross, bearing the luminous face of Christ.

The second:[62] Man is resting, and sadness possesses him as he contemplates his fate. Black clouds hide the blue sky. As they come nearer they disintegrate and reveal themselves as demons. Man falls down in terror and as he lies prostrate his arms are stretched out so that his body forms a cross. Now the horrible creatures of Hell disappear, and man knows that only Christ remains, since he is the only spirit that has passed through the Cross. If we allow our mind to dwell on this poem, we realize that the black clouds which change into demons are nothing but our own dark thoughts which change into forces that would annihilate us. The effort of concentration necessary to grasp the essence of such images will bar them to all those who do not feel that the reward is worth the labor.

In the poetry of Steffen there is no brilliance of wit, no appeal to the emotions, no attempt to charm or startle by outstanding beauty of form. The presentation is unobtrusive, the subjects, while grand and deep, are also austere and often seem remote from common experience. Their effect upon the reader is rather curious.

*An explanation of this process is given in Rudolf Steiner's *Die Geheimwissenschaft im Umriss* (pp. 269 ff.).

He is at first hardly impressed; he may turn from them
with a slight feeling of uneasiness—not exactly of shock,
for they are gentle, but of hesitating doubt as to their
ultimate value. But the aftereffect is telling. These poems
cling to the memory. They take possession of some inner
chamber of the mind where they stay and have their
being. They are alive.

Having attained a high degree of selflessness, Steffen
does not describe any part of his surroundings for the
sake of the impression it makes on him, nor is he in-
terested in giving his readers pleasurable experiences by
his presentation. *Alles Vergängliche ist nur ein Gleichnis*
—"all transient things are but symbols"—these words
from the last lines of Goethe's *Faust* might be the motto
of Steffen's lyrics. Wherever he describes, his objects
immediately become transparent, revealing eternal
meaning.

In considering his output as a whole, we see that he
has carried out his own precept: with him the approach
to poetry is conscious. Weinheber also postulates the
necessity of such an approach, but without being able to
suit his action to the idea. Inevitably the question arises:
is this procedure artificial? Will not a too-conscious
effort destroy the process of poetic growth, just as a
frost nips the tender shoot from a germinating seed?
This opinion is widespread. However, it is justified only
if the discipline involved has in it genuinely destructive
elements. In practice this appears not to be the case here.
On the contrary, the old methods of exploration adapted
by Steffen to the needs of modern man are precisely
designed to make a human being enter fully into the
process of growth itself. One point must again be
stressed: the exercises he outlines are not in themselves
meant to be creative. They are so-to-speak setting-up

exercises, which bring about a clearing, a flexibility of the mind, a readiness to receive unclouded any impression that may come to it; in fact, a strengthening of the very faculties of creation that may at first sight seem to be endangered by it.

There is no doubt that Steffen's deliberate effort toward conscious creation has colored his lyric output. The main consequence is that his poems are unified in character. This makes for a certain limitation in range, although there is to counterbalance it an increase in depth and impetus.

His chief message is a belief in the inherent power of each human being—a power that must be activated for good purposes; if activated in the wrong direction it will become destructive. Like the Expressionists, like Weinheber, and to a certain degree also Carossa, Steffen feels that an old order is coming to an end. He is like Rilke in seeing that the possibility of salvation rests with man. But he goes farther than Rilke in his intimate sympathy with all creatures of the earth, feeling that they look to man for help. What distinguishes him from his predecessors and contemporaries is his definite Christian orientation.

For a philosophy of life such as Steffen's, present political happenings are only one more scene in a cosmic drama of forces. He deliberately refrains from anything that might look like direct comment on the current manifestations of this gigantic struggle. He would influence his fellow man only to bend all his powers toward a rebirth of the world in the spirit.

CONCLUSION

IN the beginning of this study certain problems were raised: a possible contrast of conscious Weltanschauung with the visible world depicted in the poet's work; the author's stand with regard to the immediate political scene; the contribution contained in his work; and finally, the direction of his search for essential reality.

Such questions are like fishermen's nets cast into the deep. A certain catch is hoped for, but when the net comes up we must take what we find in it. The answers are often not direct; they sometimes bear obliquely on the subject posed, not quite revealing what was looked for but unexpectedly giving other light.

In a final analysis of the material it seems clear that all three poets have been deeply influenced by a background vaster than the range embraced in any single life span, more comprehensive than current happenings: the dark trend of European history and the part that forces seen directing it appear to play in the fate of mankind. These forces are felt to be at work not only in man's social development but also in that of the earth and all its creatures.

While these influences have been strong upon all three poets, their reactions differ according to the character and individual setting of each man, which condition the elements out of which they build their world and the contribution they are able to make to their time. Roughly, all belong to the same generation—the "lost generation," so called. All three lived through the first World War as grown men, and the second finds them in full possession of their creative faculties, with a background of considered philosophy of life. In 1940 Albert

Steffen had reached his fifty-sixth year, Carossa being older by six years and Weinheber eight years younger.

The great panorama forming the more or less conscious basis for the work of these poets reaches far into the past. It may be defined as a succession of disastrous national experiences, stretching back to the seventeenth century and the destruction left in the wake of the Thirty Years' War—extending through the Napoleonic upsets and the complete débâcle of the first World War, to be climaxed by the present war and events leading up to it. This sequence of desolation was broken by short and deceptive periods of brilliance following the Seven Years' War of Frederick the Great and the Franco-Prussian conflict of 1870–71.

During the last three decades of the nineteenth century, and until 1919, there were really two Germanies: the official one, which trumpeted unceasingly the glories of victory over the French archenemy—in which the army was paramount and the Kaiser's birthday the highest festival; and an unofficial one, where disillusioned men weighed the evidence of the past and saw tragedy steadily approaching a nation living in artificial optimism. These farsighted persons were powerless to influence the fate of the nation; indeed, their voices died in the public fanfare. Their apprehension formed a background of gloom for the more current, unthinking and superficial optimistic views.

The pessimistic attitudes which came to the surface after the last war are deep-rooted and not confined to Germany. They have borne dismal fruit in France, and no European country is free from them. The outstanding exponent of a philosophy grown on such soil is Oswald Spengler, whose *Decline of the West* fascinated its readers when it appeared in 1919. Cultures, according to

Spengler, are great flowers on the tree of humanity: they grow, they mature, they fade, and the flower of western culture is fading even now.

This tired and disillusioned outlook is not everywhere clearly focused, but it makes possible men like Carossa with his philosophy of patient waiting in the face of an intolerable situation. There is in him, however, a sturdy and sane quality which gives him courage to endure and to preserve the values he believes in through a time of acute danger, even though he must know that many will misunderstand his motives and doubt his integrity.

Weinheber, absorbed in his art and not prepared by his education to take part in the life of a group, does not feel the social responsibility that would be natural to a citizen of a democratic country; in fact, he would probably deny that he belongs to any group or is responsible to anything outside the realm of art and language. The stimulus this poet receives from his surroundings is an intense feeling for the ultimate destruction of everything—a destruction that something in his nature welcomes.

Albert Steffen, viewing the scene as a neutral, has necessarily a better vantage point than the other two. If he refrains from comment on contemporary events, it is by deliberate choice. He has a deep faith in the message he brings, feeling within himself its power to counteract the ills of the world. And he is imbued with the idea that the poet must be a prophet and teacher to his time, laboring for a far future.

If national tiredness and pessimism are very difficult to understand for a people whose solid optimism has developed through a long history of pioneering and democratic achievement rather than by ephemeral and deceptive victories, it becomes still more difficult for an American even to imagine that other facet of impending doom: the decline of earth itself. The faith of man in his physical universe has been instinctive for ages. But here, quite literally, the infinite power of recuperation within the forces of life is no longer taken for granted. Disintegration, seen in the social sphere, is also sensed in the very processes of earth.

This feeling is foreshadowed in the scene of Goethe's *Faust* where, after the destruction of the "beautiful world," the only remaining hope is that man may rebuild it in spirit. It is glimpsed in the feeling of disintegrating reality so evident in the Expressionists who, unable to discover new values, substitute for them strange worlds of their own imagination. Poignantly Rilke describes, in the *Duino Elegies*, his experience of the "dwindling outer world," and his intuition finds the same remedy as Goethe: Man will build an invisible world of the spirit in his soul.

Our three poets react differently to the atmosphere created by these traditions. Carossa's conscious and acute love of the earth may well be the outcome of a secret feeling of uncertainty. He does protest a great deal. His deliberate clinging to earth is not naïve—it is a hard-won attitude, by no means secure, yet valiantly maintained. Weinheber on the other hand, predisposed to pessimism by an unhappy life, embraces the dark trend without effort to overcome or balance it. He sings the beauty of doomed values; courage and nobility are of no avail against the surge of destruction.

Both attitudes are quite different from that of Steffen, who faces the issue calmly and clearly. Where Weinheber submits in somber ecstasy to the forces of annihilation, and Carossa gropes for a constructive solution, while keeping his view of reality slightly blurred, Steffen focuses the full strength of his resources on the issue in a deliberate and disciplined way.

The effect of these differences is clearly felt in their poetry. The dreamlike and floating character of Carossa's style corresponds to the uncertainty in his basic conceptions. Weinheber's poetic world reflects his emotional one: the lovely landscapes he paints are suffused with an unreal light, while ugliness is sharply defined. Although he evolves a theory of conscious creation to replace the old "intuitive" way, his poetry is not a departure but rather a brilliant symposium of many past styles.

Steffen, on the other hand, has made a definite step toward a new style in poetry, foreshadowed in Weinheber's theory but not accomplished. To the casual reader his work appears to have less literary value than that of the other two poets. But it is only natural in the evolution of a new style that the first to use it must fashion the tool; other generations of poets may extend it to broader and more perfect use.

The crux of Steffen's innovation is the deliberate discarding of what is commonly called intuition for a disciplined and conscious form of creation. Or perhaps it would be truer to say that intuition is no longer to be used haphazardly but in a firm blend with clarified mind and will. Steffen feels that in order to convey his message he must evolve a style adequate to it, and this is perforce new. The Swiss poet has not attained literary perfection and perhaps, indeed, stylistic smoothness is not in the character of this kind of poetry. For it is a poetry of realization, of meaning and sequences of meaning, rather than of words or music. But he breaks loose from all influences of which he is aware, and his style is original

in its very simplicity. The greatest difficulty facing him
is the fact that appreciation of his output presupposes in
the reader a discipline similar to that of the writer. But
in Steffen's conception, discipline and conscious effort
are the means for a possible rise of mankind from the
disintegration of our time.

Of his poetry one might say, therefore, that in the
degree to which man tends to develop these much
needed qualities, a broadening basis of appreciation will
be there.

The direction of Steffen's effort is entirely Christian,
and this is the positive source of its strength. Neither
Weinheber nor Carossa has a definite stand with regard
to the Christian faith, although both were brought up
under the influence of the Catholic Church. It is worthy
of note that also Dr. Steiner, friend and teacher of
Albert Steffen, was in his youth a Catholic. That Wein-
heber is intellectually somewhat oriented to a Christian
background is clear, but while he does not deny the
"gentle message," neither does he feel that it has power
to overcome the forces of destruction. He does not, in
fact, find rest in any abiding values, for he sees even his
own cherished reality of language going down "to be
devoured by the day." As for the saints, and Christ, they
have withdrawn from the earth and our love cannot
reach them any more. The hopelessness with which he
views life is manifest also here.

Carossa is another case. The mystic impulse is with
him a genuine thing. There are no specific allusions in
his work to Christian teaching, however; his cosmic
visions deal with undefined "powers" and the "great
spirit of mankind." His spontaneous inclination toward
mysticism is that of a medieval saint and does not indi-

cate either an interest in the springs of doctrine or an effort toward new departures. The dualism between this inclination and his resolute pursuit of the normal and the earthly is never quite resolved. In spite of his idea of cycles and of sublimation, he does not achieve a unity between the "great spiritual elements" and reality, though he labors toward that goal.

For Albert Steffen the sacrificial death and the resurrection of Christ are a most vivid personal faith. His life has been oriented to it, and his whole philosophy centers around it, pervading his poetic work. He feels, just as Rilke and Weinheber do, that the life forces are ebbing; new life can only flow into the world if man, identified with the reality of Christ by an act of free will, achieves also a unity of feeling with the earth and all its creatures. The union with Christ may be accomplished by taking the Lord's Supper—an exoteric way, or by the discipline of the mystic—an esoteric way. The unity with nature which will bring new life to the earth can only be accomplished by love and by the sacrifice of all egotistic purposes. These processes must be fully realized in consciousness, and Steffen feels this to be the only way in which modern man, as a free individual, can achieve salvation.

Here man does not find himself "between the gods and the demons" but rather between two basic and common dangers inherent in the life of mankind and of every individual: that of supreme egotism, with resulting isolation of the human being from his fellow man, and that of corroding doubt or listless despair, coupled either with cynical pleasure in the senselessness of life or with a thoughtless pursuit of anything that will bring forgetfulness. Only by constant watch can man strike a just balance between these two exaggerations in the use of his own forces—and this balance is the true secret of wholesome growth.

The apprehension of a danger sweeping down on mankind like a dark current is strong in all three poets. And so pervading an influence cannot be without significance to all who care for future development in our world. If the fear of ebbing vitality seems unreal or morbid to those bred in the peaceful air of a long-undisturbed continent, perhaps that in itself is the answer: a spirit that is as yet in the main unbroken may help to find the solution while there is still time.

NOTES AND BIBLIOGRAPHY

NOTES

1. Heinrich Heine, 1797–1856; Theodor Storm, 1817–88; Gottfried Keller, 1819–90; Conrad Ferdinand Meyer, 1825–98; Eduard Mörike, 1804–75.
2. Gerhart Hauptmann, born in 1862.
3. Hugo von Hofmannsthal, 1874–1929.
4. Georg Trakl, 1887–1914.
5. August Stramm, 1874–1915.
6. Georg Heym, 1887–1912.
7. Franz Werfel, born in 1890.
8. Stefan George, 1868–1933.
9. Rainer Maria Rilke, 1875–1926.
10. Hans Carossa, *Kindheit und Jugend* (Leipzig, 1934), p. 85.
11. *Ibid.*, p. 249.
12. *Führung und Geleit* (Leipzig, 1936), p. 169. "Dabei spürte ich deutlich, dass irgend etwas in meiner Natur diesem frommen Vorsatz immer heimlich widersprach; und was weiss man auch am Ende von sich selber?"
13. *Die Schicksale des Doktor Bürger* (Leipzig), Nr. 334.
14. *Der Arzt Gion*, Leipzig, 1937.
15. *Ibid.*, p. 54. "Sie muss erhalten bleiben, und es käme nur darauf an, sich selber so stark, so rein zu bewahren, dass man sie zu binden vermöchte ohne ihren heimlichen Kristall zu trüben. Man spricht von Engels-Ehen und sagt, sie könnten leicht zu Teufels-Ehen werden; aber vielleicht müsste man doch eine solche Heirat mit ihr wagen, bis sie zum Menschlichen erwacht. Emerenz aber ist unter tausend Weibern eine, die wieder guten Glaubens, guten Willens, ein Menschenkind zur Welt gebären will."
16. *Ibid.*, p. 291. "Den Sonnenkern umglänzt von jungen Geistern, die singenden Beratungen der Mächte, die den letzten Krieg der irdischen Gewalten vorbereiten, den glühenden Chor der kosmischen Artistinnen, die stündlich millionenmal ihre Lichtbälle in den Raum werfen und wieder auffangen müssen, ohne einen einzigen zu verfehlen, damit endlich das Reich der Kraft und Liebe zu uns komme."
17. *Geheimnisse des reifen Lebens*, Leipzig, 1936.
18. *Ibid.*, p. 148. "Ihre Heilung verdanke sie Barbaras kräftigem Beistand, zum grossen Teil aber auch, kaum wage sie es auszusprechen, den Tieren. Jedes neue Geschöpf, dem sie sich gewidmet, habe ihr ein anderes altes Gewicht von der Seele genommen."
19. *Ibid.*, p. 111. "Ihr Ziel ist ja ein ähnliches, wie es jahrelang das meinige gewesen: die Überwindung des Todes durch Verachtung des Lebens, die volle Ledigkeit der Seele, das wasserklare Ohne-Schicksal-Sein."
20. *Kindheit und Jugend*, p. 330. "Ja, wie man den bitteren Mandelbaum in

einen süssen umwandeln könne, sobald man ihm einen Teil seiner Säfte entzöge, so würden dem Fastenden gar bald Gesichte und Verzückungen zuteil, von denen sich der satte Mensch nichts träumen lasse."

21. *Geheimnisse des reifen Lebens*, p. 44. "Habe wirklich auch ich mir die Lehre vom geduldvollen Schauen gepredigt? Ich glaube, sie gehört nicht mehr zu mir. Wäre mir geholfen, würde ich ein anderer, wenn mir auf einmal im Seelenfinster die hellen Urbilder der Wesen begegneten? Vielleicht ist uns überhaupt nicht bestimmt, unmittelbar die Dinge zu erkennen, und wir sollten den Gläubigen folgen, die nur durch das kristallene Herz eines Erlösers hindurch den Blick darauf richten. Oder gibt es für uns abseits Wandelnde noch etwas anderes, Erhebungen, ungesuchte, die in Sekunden vorwegnehmen, was aller Fleiss der Jahre nicht erreicht?"

22. *Führung und Geleit*, p. 130. "In verwandter Gefahr empfinden sich viele gegenüber den grossen geistigen Elementen. Sie halten sich von ihnen fern und decken sie ihr Leben lang mit Nicht-Wissen zu, so wie wir Phosphor unter Wasser bewahren, damit kein Brand entsteht."

23. *Ibid.*, p. 96. "Von Rodin habe er gelernt, einen Baum, ein Tier, eine Statue, einen Menschen oder auch eine überlieferte Figur der Geschichte so oft und so eindringlich anzusehen, bis auf einmal eine wesenhafte Erscheinung des Betrachteten in ihm auftauchte. Ganz unbekannt war mir diese Verfahrungsart nicht; ein kleiner anthroposophischer Aufsatz, der mir vor Augen gekommen, sagte das nämliche aus; doch hielt ich solche geistigen Schulungen für viel zu schwierig und langwierig, um sie etwa mir selber zuzutrauen."

24. *Geheimnisse des reifen Lebens*, p. 8.

25. *Kindheit und Jugend*, p. 173. "Und sonderbar: oft hat er zum Himmel geblickt, bei Tag und bei Nacht, und immer war es herrlich; aber nie ist ihm dabei das Unermessliche so tief ins Gefühl gegangen wie vor diesen künstlichen Flächen mit Sternenpunkten und fremden Bezeichnungen."

26. *Gesammelte Gedichte* (Leipzig, 1938), p. 59.

27. *Geheimnisse des reifen Lebens*, p. 99.

28. *Ibid.*, p. 25.

29. *Ibid.*, p. 59.

30. *Ibid.*, pp. 104 ff.

31. *Ibid.*, pp. 179 ff.

32. *Ibid.*, p. 182. "Bewahre sich jeder tief innen eine streng umschwiegene Zelle! Da mögen aus Leiden und Glück die Gedanken wachsen, die das Nährsalz der Zukunft sind, auch wenn sie niemals aufgeschrieben werden."

33. Josef Weinheber, *Persönlichkeit und Schaffen*, herausgegeben von Adolf Luser, Wien-Leipzig, 1935. ". . . ein Zuhause, das, ferne und besser als das Wirkliche, im Geiste beruht. Dort sind erlauchte Namen gereiht um ein allein gelassenes Herz: Alkaios und Sappho, Mark Aurel und Schopenhauer, Hölderlin und die Droste. Sie sind zuletzt, über meine Vaterstadt hinaus, meine unzerstörbare Heimat; über meine Väter hinaus, meine unverlierbare Ahnenschaft."

34. *Adel und Untergang* (München, 1934), p. 37.
35. *Zwischen Göttern und Dämonen*, München, 1938.
36. *Persönlichkeit und Schaffen*, p. 60. "Nicht der menschliche Geist, sondern die geheimnisvolle Möglichkeit, ihm in der Sprache Körper und Figur zu verleihen, unterscheidet den Menschen von der 'stummen' Kreatur. Und allein die Sprache könnte ihn zu dem Anspruch berechtigen, sich jenen gegenüber als höheres Wesen anzusehen. Die Sprache ist die Wirklichkeit des Geistigen, und durch sie wird der Mensch eine geistige Wirklichkeit."
    "Nun aber diese Wirklichkeit der Menschheit nicht als Einheitliches gegeben ist . . . sondern in Idiome zerfällt, bedeutet das Idiom den Ausdruck jenes menschheitlichen Teilwesens, welches als Volk, und unter gewissen Umständen als Nation in die Erscheinung tritt. Volk ist eine vitale Wirklichkeit, die ihm angehörende Sprache seine geistige Natur." "In der Sprache liegt Schicksal, Vergangenheit und jeglicher geistiger Besitz eines Volkes aufbewahrt und beschlossen. Ein Volk verliert seine Würde nicht durch verlorene Kriege, sondern durch den Verfall seiner Sprache, und der eigentliche Hochverräter ist der Sprachverderber."
    "Dieser höchste Wert nun, den ein Volk besitzt . . . ist als geistiges Gut seinen Dichtern anvertraut."
37. *Adel und Untergang*, p. 100. (Compare the poem "Voyelles" by the French Symbolist, Arthur Rimbaud.)
38. *Persönlichkeit und Schaffen*, pp. 41 ff.
39. Alfred Rosenberg, *Der Mythus des zwanzigsten Jahrhunderts*, München, 1935 (published first, 1930). "Das Wesen der heutigen Weltrevolution liegt im Erwachen der rassischen Typen," p. 479.
40. *Ibid.*, p. 531. "Die stärkste Persönlichkeit ruft heute nicht mehr nach Persönlichkeit, sondern nach Typus."
41. *Ibid.*, p. 539. "Individualismus und Universalismus sind . . . Weltanschauungen des Verfalls. . . ."
42. *Ibid.*, p. 564. "Wir kennen und erleben endlich heute die Mächte der aus tiefem Schlaf erwachenden Rassenseele. . . ."
43. Hermann Pongs, *Josef Weinheber, Zwischen Göttern und Dämonen* (Dichtung und Volkstum), Vol. XL, Pt. 1, pp. 77–84.
44. *Kammermusik* (München, 1939), p. 65.
45. *Späte Krone* (München, 1936), p. 109.
46. *Ibid.*, p. 113.
47. *Begegnungen mit Rudolf Steiner* (Zürich-Leipzig, 1926), p. 12: "Um das Leben in allen Abgründen zu durchdringen, quartierte ich mich in eine Gasse ein, wo Elend und Verkommenheit herrschten. Mein Zimmer ging auf einen Hinterhof, in den die Türen einer düsteren Spelunke mündeten. Nachts drang das Gejohle und Gekreische der Insassen ununterbrochen zu mir herauf. . . ."
    "Ich vernahm aus diesem inneren Laut den Untergang der Seele. Es war wie ein Hilferuf, ein Anklammern . . . , wie eine heftig dringende Mahnung, das Wort der Erlösung zu finden."

48. Rudolf Steiner, *Knowledge of the Higher Worlds and Its Attainment*, Anthroposophic Press, New York, 1931. For numerous other works see publications of the Anthroposophic Press, 225 West 57th Street, New York City.

49. *Der Künstler zwischen Westen und Osten* (Zürich-Leipzig, 1925), pp. 256 ff.

50. *Buch der Rückschau* (Dornach, 1939), pp. 168 ff.

51. *Der Tröster* (Dornach, 1936), p. 38.

52. *Ibid.*, p. 44.

53. *Ibid.*, p. 29.

54. *Wegzehrung*, p. 134.

55. *Ibid.*, p. 158.

56. *Ibid.*, p. 35.

57. *Ibid.*, p. 130.

58. *Ibid.*, p. 130.

59. See Erika von Erhardt-Siebold, "Mediaeval Windows in Romantic Light," *Essays and Studies in Honor of Carleton Brown*, New York, 1940.

60. See Alice D. Snyder, "Coleridge's Cosmogony: A Note on the Poetic World-View," *Studies in Philology*, XXI, 4, October, 1924.

61. *Wegzehrung*, p. 14.

62. *Ibid.*, p. 33.

BIBLIOGRAPHY

Works by Hans Carossa

Stella Mystica, Traum eines Toren, Berlin, 1907.
Gedichte, Leipzig, 1910, 1912, 1923, 1932.
Doktor Bürgers Ende. Letzte Blätter eines Tagebuches, Leipzig, 1913.
Die Flucht. Ein Gedicht aus Doktor Bürgers Nachlass, Leipzig, 1916.
Ostern, Gedichte, Berlin, 1920.
Eine Kindheit, Leipzig, 1922.
Rumänisches Tagebuch, Leipzig, 1924. Neuauflage, *Tagebuch im Kriege*, Leipzig, 1934.
Verwandlungen einer Jugend, Leipzig, 1931. Vereint mit *Eine Kindheit* zu *Kindheit und Jugend*, Leipzig, 1934.
Der Arzt Gion. Eine Erzählung, Leipzig, 1931.
Führung und Geleit. Ein Lebensgedenkbuch, Leipzig, 1933.
Geheimnisse des reifen Lebens, Leipzig, 1936.
Wirkungen Goethes in der Gegenwart, Leipzig, 1938.
Gesammelte Gedichte, Leipzig, 1938.
Das Jahr der schönen Täuschungen, Leipzig, 1941.

Works by Josef Weinheber

Der einsame Mensch, Wien, 1920.
Von beiden Ufern, Wien, 1923.
Das Waisenhaus. Novel, Wien, 1925.
Boot in der Bucht, Wien, 1926.
Adel und Untergang, München, 1934.
Wien wörtlich, München, 1935.
Vereinsamtes Herz, Leipzig, 1935.
Persönlichkeit und Schaffen, herausgegeben von Adolf Luser, Wien-Leipzig, 1935.
Späte Krone, München, 1936.
O Mensch gib Acht. Ein erbauliches Kalenderbuch für Stadt- und Landleut, München, 1937.
Zwischen Göttern und Dämonen, München, 1938.
Kammermusik, München, 1939.

Works by Albert Steffen

Ott, Alois und Werelsche. Novel, Berlin, 1907; also Dornach, Switzerland.

Die Bestimmung der Roheit. Novel, Berlin, 1912.

Die Erneuerung des Bundes. Novel, Berlin, 1913.

Der rechte Liebhaber des Schicksals. Novel, Berlin, 1916.

Der Auszug aus Aegypten; die Manichäer. Two dramas, Berlin, 1916.

Sybilla Mariana. Novel, Berlin, 1917.

Die Heilige mit dem Fische. Short stories, Berlin, 1919.

Das Viergetier. Drama, published in the periodical, *Das Reich*, 1920.

Wegzehrung. Poems, Basel, 1921; also Dornach, Switzerland.

Die Krisis im Leben des Künstlers. Essays, Zürich-Leipzig, 1922; also Dornach, Switzerland.

Kleine Mythen. Zürich, 1923; also Dornach, Switzerland.

Hieram und Salomo. Drama, Dornach, Switzerland, 1925.

In Memoriam Rudolf Steiner. Basel, 1925; also Dornach, Switzerland.

Pilgerfahrt zum Lebensbaum. Essays, Dornach, Switzerland, 1925.

Der Künstler zwischen Westen und Osten. Essays, Zürich-Leipzig, 1925; also Dornach, Switzerland.

Begegnungen mit Rudolf Steiner. Sketches, Zürich-Leipzig, 1926; also Dornach, Switzerland.

Der Chef des Generalstabs. Drama, Dornach, Switzerland, 1927.

Lebensgeschichte eines jungen Menschen. Novel, Dornach, Switzerland, 1928.

Der Künstler und die Erfüllung der Mysterien. Essays, Dornach, Switzerland, 1928.

Der Sturz des Antichrist. Dramatical sketch, Dornach, Switzerland, 1928.

Wildeisen. Novel, Dornach, Switzerland, 1929.

Mani (Sein Leben und seine Lehre), Dornach, Switzerland, 1930.

Lebenswende. Short stories, Dornach, Switzerland, 1931.

Sucher nach sich selbst. Novel, Switzerland, 1931.

Gedichte. Poems, Dornach, Switzerland, 1931.

Goethes Geistgestalt. Essays, Dornach, Switzerland, 1932.

Das Todeserlebnis des Manes. Drama, Dornach, Switzerland, 1934.

Adonisspiel, Eine Herbstfeier. Drama, Dornach, Switzerland, 1935.
Der Tröster. Poems, Dornach, Switzerland, 1936.
Friedenstragödie. Drama, Dornach, Switzerland, 1936.
Im andern Land—In Another Land. Poems intertranslated, Dornach, Switzerland, 1937.
Fahrt ins andere Land. Drama, Dornach, Switzerland, 1938.
Buch der Rückschau. Autobiographic sketches, Dornach, Switzerland, 1939.
Lebensbild Pestalozzis. Biography, Dornach, Switzerland, 1939.
Pestalozzi. Drama, Dornach, Switzerland, 1939.
Passiflora—Ein Requiem. Dornach, Switzerland, 1939.
Frührot der Mysteriendichtung. Essays, Dornach, Switzerland, 1940.
Selbsterkenntnis und Lebensschau. Autobiographic sketches, Dornach, Switzerland, 1940.

Works of Reference

(As this book deals with a special aspect of lyric poetry, many works dealing with other aspects are left out.)

General

A. Barthels, *Geschichte der deutschen Literatur*, Hamburg, 1934.
P. Fechter, *Deutsche Dichtung der Gegenwart*, Reclam, 1930.
H. Kindermann, *Das literarische Antlitz der Gegenwart*, Halle, 1930.
F. Koch, *Geschichte der deutschen Dichtung*, Hamburg, 1937.
E. Kretschmar, *Goethe und Rilke*, Dresden, 1937.
W. Mahrholz, *Deutsche Literatur der Gegenwart*, Reclam, 1930.
E. Morwitz, *Die Dichtung Stefan Georges*, Berlin, 1934.
J. Nadler, *Literaturgeschichte der deutschen Stämme und Landschaften*, Regensburg, 1912 ff.
A. Soergl, *Dichtung und Dichter der Zeit. Im Banne des Expressionismus*, Leipzig, 1927.

Hans Carossa

L. F. Bartel, *Um Hans Carossa*, Völkische Kultur, April, 1934.
Buch des Dankes für Carossa, 15. Dezember 1928, Leipzig, 1928.
K. Graucob, *Hans Carossas Selbstdarstellungen seiner Kindheit*, Zeitschrift für angewandte Psychologie, Vol. XLIV, Pt. 3 & 4, 1932.

M. Greiner, *Die Dichtung Hans Carossas*, Zeitschrift für Deutsch-
kunde, Vol. XLV, Pt. 1, 1931.

A. Haueis, *Hans Carossa, Persönlichkeit und Werk*, Weimar, 1935.

O. E. Hesse, *Hans Carossa, Ein Bekenntnis*, Tübingen, 1932.

F. Klatt, *Hans Carossa, seine geistige Haltung und sein Glaubensgut*,
Stuttgart-Leipzig, 1937.

M. Machate, *Hans Carossa*, Diss. Münster, i.W., 1934.

K. Nadler, *Symbol und Existenz im dichterischen Kunstwerk Hans
Carossas*, Dichtung und Volkstum, Vol. XL, Pt. 2, 1934.

F. Pongs, *Krieg als Volksschicksal im neuen Schrifttum*, Euphorion,
Vol. XXXV, Pt. 1, 1934.

M. Thiessen, *Das Ich bei Rilke und Carossa*, Amsterdam, 1935.

Josef Weinheber

F. Koch, *Josef Weinheber*, Zeitschrift für Deutschkunde, Vol. XLIX,
Pt. 7, 1935.

H. Pongs, *Josef Weinheber: Zwischen Göttern und Dämonen*,
Dichtung und Volkstum, Vol. XL, Pt. 1, 1939.

Josef Weinheber, *Persönlichkeit und Schaffen*, Leipzig, 1935.

Albert Steffen

A. von Sybel-Petersen, *Albert Steffen und sein Werk*, Basel, 1934.

Date Due
